...ISBOURG HERITAGE:
From Ruins to Reconstruction

Louisbourg Heritage

From Ruins to Reconstruction

TERRY MACLEAN

UCCB Press

University College of Cape Breton Press
Box 5300
Sydney, Nova Scotia
CANADA B1P 6L2

Cover photos: 1945 postcard of the Louisbourg ruins superimposed on a 1989 aerial photo of the Louisbourg reconstruction. Source: Postcard photo courtesy of the Beaton Institute, University College of Cape Breton, aerial photo courtesy of the Fortress of Louisbourg National historic Site (Parks Canada).
Book design by B. Berry, Goose Lane Editions
Printed and bound in Canada by Advocate Printing, Pictou, Nova Scotia

Canadian Cataloguing in Publication Data

MacLean, Terry, 1946-
    Louisbourg heritage
    Includes bibliographical references.
    ISBN 0-920336-62-0

1. Fortress of Louisbourg National Historic Park (N.S.) — History.
2. Historic sites — Nova Scotia — Louisbourg — Conservation and restoration.
3. Historic preservation — Nova Scotia — Louisbourg.   I. title.

FC2314 L68M33 1995   971.6'955   C94-950267-7
F1039.5.L8M33 1995

Dedicated to my mother,
Evangeline
and sons,
Trevor and Jeffrey

Preface

This book is based on my work with Parks Canada from 1970 to 1981, my studies at the University of Leicester, Department of Museum Studies and my research and teaching as a member of the faculty at the University College of Cape Breton since 1981. I would like to acknowledge the help given to me by all three institutions and by the many individuals who have sustained me in these efforts. Special thanks are due to Dr. Robert J. Morgan, a colleague and a very close personal friend who has encouraged and supported me throughout my career in public history and museums, especially when I needed it most. I acknowledge the independent review and editing of Mr. David Smythe, UCCB Department of Culture, Heritage and Lesuire Studies and Penny Marshall, University College Librarian and Executive Director, UCCB Press. The errors are my responsibility.

My work has also been based on visits to the Louisbourg ruins since childhood, to many other museums and historic sites as an adult and on a life-long interest in historical scholarship and fiction. For this study and for the personal satisfaction derived from these visits, I owe a debt of gratitude to the staff members and countless visitors who talked with me and to the many authors and artists who wrote about and illustrated these very special places in history.

Contents

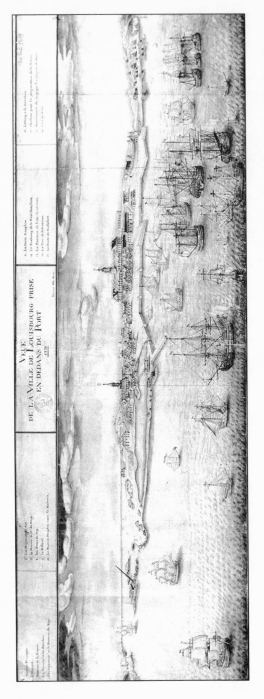

1731 View Veue de la Ville de Louisbourg Prise En Dedans du Port. This view, drawn by Verrier *fils*, son of the Chief Engineer of the colony from a ship in the harbour. It provides a representation of Louisbourg as a trading centre and the capital of Isle Royale. Source: FRANCE, BIBLIOTHEQUE NATIONALE

Introduction

Louisbourg History and Museology

In the preface to the internationally best-selling book *Sarum: The Novel of England*, Edward Rutherfurd wrote:

> No place in England, I believe, has a longer visible history of building and occupation than the Sarum region. The wealth of archaeological information, let alone historical record, is so overwhelming that even a novelist, wishing to convey the full story of the place would have to write a book three or four times as long as I have done.[1]

Rutherfurd wrote more than a thousand pages in his novel about the Salisbury Plain and what it has meant as a special place in English history. His method was to select accurate information in a personal way and hope that in doing so he "may have conveyed something of the wonder of the place."[2]

---

1   Edward Rutherfurd, *Sarum: The Novel of England*, Random House Canada edition, Toronto, Ballantine Books, 1987, preface.

2   Ibid.

In Canadian terms the Fortress of Louisbourg National Historic Site, even with its much more recent and compact history and a more circumscribed though rich historiography, has become a similarly well documented and special place. In their work historians, archaeologists, builders and interpreters have selected information and presented their version of the history of the place to the public in the form of a physical and visual reconstruction supplemented by words and illustrations. That was their method and the general public was their audience, just as literature and the general reader guided Rutherfurd's attempt to represent Sarum. The Louisbourg method and the results are the subject of this book, which attempts to describe and assess the project as a case study and model in public history; as comparable to a good historical novel or film as it is to an academic treatise or scholarly monograph.

Another successful author of historical fiction, James Clavell, wrote in the frontispiece of *Gai-Jin: A Novel of Japan*:

> It is not history but fiction. Many of the happenings did occur according to historians and to books of history, which, of themselves, do not necessarily always relate what truly happened . . . I have played with history — the where and how and who and why and when of it — to suit my own reality and, perhaps, to tell the real history of what came to pass.[3]

Historical fiction, history museums and historic sites, historical restorations and reconstructions, art galleries and even theme parks make an important contribution to the public's understanding of particular aspects of the past, though they often distort it. They increase our appreciation for the importance and the significance of history and its manifestations in our present landscape and con-

---

3   James Clavell, *Gai-Jin: A Novel of Japan*, New York, Delacorte Press, 1993, frontispiece.

sciousness, thereby justifying and creating a market for costly preservation efforts in many countries.

The Canadian experience is more recent and isolated, largely because of colonial status and regional differences in geography and political culture. Canadian writers of historical fiction and scholarship began to flourish after the second World War. The museum and historical preservation movement gradually began to take shape after 1950. That progress in what could be termed "public history" reached its apogee in the 1960's in the years preceding and following Canadian Centennial celebrations in 1967. Research and development at Louisbourg, spanning the years 1961 to 1981, constituted by far the largest undertaking in the Canadian heritage field at that time and was one of the largest of its kind in the western world.

Louisbourg History

The French town, harbour and fortifications at Louisbourg had a brief but significant history. The eighteenth-century colony of Isle Royale, which comprised present-day Cape Breton and Prince Edward Island, was established in 1713 after Newfoundland was ceded to the British by the Treaty of Utrecht. Additional territorial losses in Acadia left the French with Cape Breton as the best base for their lucrative cod fishery. Louisbourg became capital of the new colony in 1718 and soon developed as the east coast trading centre for all of New France and a strategic military and naval base for the Gulf of St. Lawrence and Quebec.[4]

Louisbourg's importance was indicated by the decision to build

---

4   Christopher Moore, "The Maritime Economy of Isle Royale,"
    Canada, An Historical Magazine, Vol. 1, No. 4 (June 1, 1974), pp.
    32-46.

extensive fortifications and sea batteries to protect the town and harbour. Construction was continuous from the early 1720s until the outbreak of war in 1744. New England colonists supported by the British fleet successfully attacked Louisbourg in 1745 and occupied the town until 1749, when Cape Breton was returned to France after the Treaty of Aix-La-Chapelle. The French strengthened the fortifications during the early 1750s and continued to use the port as a base for the French navy, but Louisbourg was again besieged successfully in 1758 by more than 13,000 British troops under the command of Major-General Geoffrey Amherst, with substantial fleet support from the Royal Navy. The British destroyed the fortifications in 1760 and abandoned Louisbourg after the Seven Years War (1756-63) in favour of Halifax, established in 1749 as the capital of the British colony of Nova Scotia and one of the principal overseas bases for the Royal Navy.

Louisbourg is remembered by many as the site of these two important battles, but its historical significance is not limited to military affairs. As a trading centre and base of operations for the North Atlantic fishery, France's loss of Louisbourg in 1758 was a very serious setback economically as well as militarily. Louisbourg, is best understood as a fortified French port on the east coast of North America in frequent and regular contact with the major port cities of France, especially Rochefort and La Rochelle. Its orientation was coastal and European, unlike many of the French possessions in the interior which developed on the basis of North American resources such as agriculture and the fur trade. Louisbourg depended on the sea. Its strategic location on the Atlantic ocean determined its role in direct relationship to France's economic and military interests in Europe and in the rest of North America.

Because of its brief and compact history, Louisbourg has provided the basis for fascinating and varied studies of eighteenth century French culture transplanted to North America. Unlike all other substantial and significant colonial sites, Louisbourg has no major continuum into the nineteenth and twentieth centuries, no city built over it. The consequence in historical, archaeological and museological terms has been a unique and extraordinary opportunity to preserve, study and describe the material culture and life of an important eighteenth century community.

Louisbourg Historiography & Early Museology

Two hundred years elapsed between abandonment of Louisbourg by the French and British and major development of its remains as a Canadian historic site, but its historical significance was recognized throughout the intervening period. The ruins were visited and written about continuously by small numbers of informed visitors, and there is an extensive historiography on Louisbourg in scholarship and fiction throughout the nineteenth century (see bibliography).

Active commemoration of its history began at Louisbourg in 1895 with the commemoration of the 150th anniversary of the first siege and culminated in the designation of Louisbourg as a National Historical Site in 1928.

Although the ruins were a fascination to visitors from the middle to the late nineteenth century, there is no evidence of public appeals for preservation of the ruins or for official commemoration of Louisbourg people and events. Though Britain, France and the United States had developed significant heritage preservation movements and extensive museum institutions by this time, Canada as a very young nation had not. A further explanation has been offered, one which underlines the special qualities of Louisbourg as a place in history:

> Given the romanticism of the era, the absence of calls to protect or clean up the site is not too surprising. It was precisely the juxtaposition of old ruins with fences, fish flakes [large wooden racks for drying codfish], houses and shops, the contrast of a glorious past with a humble present, that so captivated visitors.[5]

Louisbourg received its first memorial in 1895, not from Canada but from the United States. A 26-foot high column was erected just outside the King's Bastion ruins to mark the 150th anniversary of the successful New England siege in 1745. Soon there were several expressions of concern for the preservation of the Louisbourg ruins, but they were isolated and largely ignored in Ottawa by a federal government without "the inclination or capability to oversee such sites."[5] This situation started to change in 1919 when the Historic Sites and Monuments Board of Canada (HSMB) was created. These were formative years for the Parks Branch of the Department of the Interior and virtually no attention was paid to historic sites.

Louisbourg was one of the first historic sites to be considered by the HSMB, but the land was privately owned, as shown in investigations carried out in 1920 and 1921. The land acquisition by the Parks Branch began in 1921 and increased its ownership to nearly 72 acres by 1924. Finally in August, 1926, Louisbourg received its first recognition from the Canadian Government with the unveiling of four commemorative on cairns written in English and French.[6]

The efforts of several dedicated and influential people, led by Senator McLennan, convinced the Government of Canada to designate Louisbourg as a National Historic Site and to appropriate funds for its development. This was not a widespread preservation movement.

In this context, the development of Louisbourg as a museum and historic site between 1928 and 1940 was at least a moderate success. As in the post-1960 period, this early development was spurred by economic realities. The 1929 stock market crash and subsequent depression creating an urgent need for worthwhile public works. Sporadic efforts to stabilize and in some cases to reconstruct masonry ruins using unskilled laborers would be judged harshly by modern preservation standards, but the principal objective of creat-

---

5   Ibid., p. 65.

6   Ibid., p. 70.

ing employment was met and some principles of museum philosophy and practice were established in the process.

As part of this effort a masonry museum was constructed in 1935-36 to protect and display objects donated to the site and artifacts recovered during excavations. It soon became an important educational centre for the Cape Breton area and competently met the challenge of interpreting the ruins of the fortress and town for 25 years. A secure and aesthetically pleasing structure, the building has survived to the present day and still plays an important role in the interpretation of a much larger Louisbourg museum and historic site to the public. The following example illustrates the high standard of museological practice set at Louisbourg in a period when relatively primitive standards of museum theory and practice prevailed in most Canadian museums of similar size and with a similar scope of collections.

The most important and educationally valuable display piece was a model of the fortress and town. Built by the museum's curator, Katherine McLennan, the surprisingly detailed and generally accurate model was based on extensive cartographic research carried out in Paris by Miss McLennan and her father, Senator McLennan, who had written a definitive history of Louisbourg, published in 1918 by Macmillan of London.[7] Both the model and the book have survived the test of more than three decades of intensive research since 1961. Until it was refurbished and returned to its original location in the old museum after the opening of the park's Visitor Reception Centre in 1977, the model served as one of the principal means of orientation for visitors to Louisbourg.[8] It succeeded in cap-

---

7 John S. McLennan, *Louisbourg From Its Foundation to Its Fall*, London: MacMillan, 1918.

8 The model was located in a small exhibit building at the edge of the interior glacis of the King's Bastion, just outside the Old Museum. Visitors would arrive by bus, line up surrounding the model and then receive an introductory orientation lecture from a park guide.

tivating and educating visitors precisely because it gave clear visual expression to the labours of historical research and stimulated their imaginations in the process.

The rest of the museum exhibits consisted of attractive display cases containing somewhat randomly selected artifacts, primarily military, simply labeled but not placed in any kind of historical context or sequence. They survived for decades and eventually became a curiosity alongside post-1960 exhibits and displays that were based on focused research, storyline development and carefully written scripts, practices that came to characterize exhibits at the most successful modern museums and education centres, including Louisbourg.

The old museum at Louisbourg was typical of small museums of its era, but superior in the Canadian context. The years of fascination by many and dedication by few left an important legacy for Katherine McLennan and those who followed her. They developed a local and national awareness of an important historic resource in an era when Canada was criticized consistently for its lack of good museums.[9] Its success was based largely on the surrounding ruins, effectively placed into context by the McLennan model. The rugged coastline, the harbour and other natural features were left to speak for themselves as reminders of important events, but they combined with the ruins to convey with considerable impact a sense of place and time. That same sense is conveyed with even greater effect today by the reconstruction and surrounding natural and historical resources.

It is this quality, the location of historical resources on the actual site of significant historical events, that has given Louisbourg a special place in Canada's national heritage. It had ensured the success of the old museum and has inspired many since the 1930's to recognize the importance of Louisbourg as an international historic site. Major development of the site since 1961 has greatly increased the public's awareness of Louisbourg's significance, but that later growth

---

9   Sir Henry Miers and S.F. Markham, "A Directory of Museums and
     Art Galleries," *Report of a Canadian Survey*, New York: The Carnegie
     Corp., 1936.

was founded on the important educational benefits of the old museum and the ruins from 1935 to 1960, especially the efforts of the curator, Katherine McLennan.

Although Louisbourg was widely appreciated for its historical significance, the principal impetus for major site development was socio-economic, not historical or cultural. Any attempt to understand the scope and the pace of the project must begin with that premise. The essential problem confronted in 1959 by government officials was the serious decline of the coal and steel industries in a local economy that lacked diversity. Displaced workers could not be absorbed elsewhere in the region. As a consequence of economic decline, social changes began to disrupt the communities of industrial Cape Breton: family members moving to more prosperous regions of Canada; labour-management relations deteriorating; recreational, cultural and intellectual activities decreasing because of the lack of disposable income for the members of the working class who formed a majority in most towns and in the only city, Sydney.

By the 1950s Canada had developed a strong tradition of government intervention in the economy. In 1950 the Royal Commission on National Development in the Arts, Letters and Science (Massey Commission) began the expansion of the federal government's role in the cultural and intellectual life of Canadians.[10] The gradual growth of this trend in subsequent decades provided the social and political climate which made possible the decision to provide federal government funds for major development of Louisbourg as a National Historic Site.

The Massey Commission in 1950 and government action on many of its recommendations, principally the creation of the Canada Council and increased financial support for universities, museums, galleries and the performing arts, marked the end of slow growth in Canadian museums. As Canada matured as a nation with strong

---

10 Right Honorable Vincent Massey (Chairman), "Canadian Museums and Art Galleries", *Report of the Royal Commission on Arts, Letters and Sciences*, Ottawa, King's Printer, 1950.

British and French traditions to counterbalance the increasing and controversial influence of American values and culture, the importance of government action as an agency of change and growth was recognized. Also, Canada as a colony and then as a young nation had lacked the level of philanthropy and support from private enterprise that so stimulated the growth of large American and British museums in the late 19th and early 20th centuries. As a result Canadian museums gradually developed as public institutions on the national and provincial level and as public, tax supported, and generally much smaller museums on the municipal level. Until the 1960s, specifically the years preceding and following Canada's centennial in 1967, the Royal Ontario Museum (ROM) in Toronto, Ontario, was the only large museum with international collections and involvements that was not owned and operated directly by the federal government.[11] Even the ROM relied increasingly on federal funding in the period of growth following the Massey Commission.

The federal government response to the serious economic problems facing Cape Breton and other Canadian coal mining districts was to appoint another Royal Commission in October, 1959, led by the Honorable I.C. Rand. The report of the Rand Royal Commission was essentially an economic analysis of the Canadian coal industry, with particular reference to Cape Breton as the country's largest coal mining district. It warrants close study as an example of how government action on economic problems can affect cultural policy, in this case historical and museological.

The Commission confirmed that economic prospects for the coal industry in Cape Breton were dismal and that a single extractive industry was not a desirable economic base for such a large community. In the spirit of cultural awareness inspired by the Massey Commission the report turned first to Cape Breton's natural and historic heritage. Describing the island as a haven of natural beauty, blessed with the "munificence of nature", the Commission urged the use of these re-

---

11 Archie F. Key, *Beyond Four Walls: The Origins and Development of Canadian Museums*, Toronto, McClelland and Stewart, 1973.

sources to stimulate the tourist industry. Since its completion in the 1930s and particularly during the 1950s, the Cabot Trail in Cape Breton Highlands National Park had already stimulated a steady increase in the number of tourists traveling to the island to view the coastline and natural beauty of the island from the northern elevations of the national park. Turning to historic resources the report focused on Louisbourg in a lengthy passage that must be quoted in full because of its later importance. It describes the turning point envisaged in the evolution of Louisbourg as a national monument:

Moldering on the southeastern coast of the Island is a mute reminder of the wastage of time. Here is the scene of one of the striking events in the historical course of things that has led to the Canada of today. In the early part of the 18th century began the work of building the strongest fortification then existing on the Atlantic Coast of North America and of establishing a community bringing to the New World the architecture, traditions and culture of the French people at the direction of the most polished court of continental Europe. As a revelation of European life of that century and a reminder of the vicissitudes of North America's development, what could be more stimulating to the imagination or instructive to the mind, not only for the people of Cape Breton and Nova Scotia, but of Canada and the eastern portion of the United States, than to look upon a symbolic reconstruction of the Fortress of Louisbourg. Not that each item in the total scene should appear, but sufficient to furnish a comprehensive representation of the material and cultural forms set up on a strange land inviting settlement. That site marks a salient occasion in the transplantation of a civilization significant to the history of Canada; and to allow it to sink into ruin and obliteration would be a grave loss to the civilizing interests of this country. [12]

---

12   Ibid., p. 47.

Two phrases are of particular importance in this study of Louisbourg as a museum and historic site. The first is the general vision of a reconstructed Fortress of Louisbourg that provided the philosophical context for general project objectives developed in the early 1960s and adhered to for two decades, despite rising costs and serious objections from proponents of preservation and restoration over reconstruction. The second phrase also makes a statement on the evolution of thinking in the Canadian preservation movement: "to allow it to sink into ruin and obliteration would be a grave loss to the civilizing interests of this country." The two decades after 1959 would see significant expansion of the preservation movement inside Parks Canada and in the country in general. The philosophies and policies discussed and refined at Louisbourg in the early 1960s made a major contribution to the development of the heritage preservation movement. Louisbourg was the first major project of its kind in Canada, and to a large extent Canadians in this field were able to broaden their interest in, and acceptance and support for, historic preservation by reference to the Louisbourg model.

> Whether the example is the Citadel in Halifax, the Historic Waterfront Properties, or some of the restorations and outdoor museums that have flourished since the 1960s, a common theme when work begins is that these towns are catching up with their history, and the Fortress of Louisbourg is often their point of comparison.[13]

The Rand Commission recommended in August, 1960, that "beginning not later than in the year 1961, work on a scheme of reconstructing the ruins of the Fortress of Louisbourg as an historic site be commenced . . ."[14] In accepting the recommendation the Federal Cabinet of Canada phrased its decision in a manner equally

---

13 John Fortier, "Louisbourg: Managing a Moment in Time," *The History of Atlantic Canada: Museum Interpretations,* Peter E. Rider (ed.), National Museum of Man Mercury Series, pp. 95-96.

as pertinent to project philosophy and objectives as the earlier Rand report statement:

> The Fortress of Louisbourg is to be restored partially so that future generations can thereby see and understand the role of the Fortress as a hinge of history. The restoration is to be carried out so that the lessons of history can be animated.[15]

The reference to animation provided another major philosophical direction to Louisbourg as an outdoor museum. It has been quoted repeatedly since 1961 as the principal basis for the development of an interpretation programme at Louisbourg that combines buildings, property features, collections and staff in period costume to produce a cultural landscape, one in which an attempt is made to provide a comprehensive and detailed interpretation of eighteenth-century Louisbourg.

---

14 Rand, *Report of the Royal Commission on Coal*, p. 53. See Appendix. 1.

15 Cabinet Minute, 1961, as quoted in John Lunn et al., Fortress of Louisbourg Interpretive Plan: A Pattern for the '70s, Manuscript on file, Fortress of Louisbourg, 1971, Part 1, p. 1.

CHAPTER 1
Early Research & Source Gathering

Though early efforts to commemorate and develop Louisbourg were inspiring, they provided little specific guidance to project staff during the initial phase of development between 1961 and 1964. Philosophical statements such as those contained in the Rand Report and strategic objectives from politicians and bureaucrats on creating employment and generating local economic benefits were insufficient as a project brief, and could not serve as the bases for integrated workplans to guide the various disciplines and occupational groups required for such a massive undertaking. That initial task of organizing work was left mainly to engineers hired for the project and they very quickly began to identify research requirements, including schedules conceived in isolation from the professionals in history and archaeology who would have to direct and carry out the actual work. This chapter will outline the early efforts to establish a research programme adapted to the requirements of engineering and construction, investigate some of the specialized methodologies developed in that process and describe the initial data base assembled for the project.

The pressure to create employment and show progress at Louisbourg was extreme, but the National Parks Branch lacked the experience necessary to launch such an ambitious project. A costly combination of consultants and new staff was soon required to complement existing expertise in engineering, restoration design and construction trades. The mix of professional, technical, and trades personnel assembled for the Louisbourg project was not out of proportion to the scope and complexity of the work required, but they had to develop in a short period of time innovative and direct lines of communication as a substitute for proper planning and coordination of assignments. It would be ten years before a comprehensive planning process was in place to guide decisions. Progress during the first decade of the project depended on a consultative process that was eventually formalized as a committee structure; a study of that process illuminates much of what was achieved and not achieved in the early years of the project, particularly by research staff and project consultants.

Initial Research Programme

The most important objective of the historical research was to supply detailed information for the archaeological excavation and subsequent reconstruction of historic properties selected for development, principally the fortifications and buildings in the King's Bastion. The deadlines imposed by archaeology and construction schedules, combined with the problems raised by the unexpectedly large extent of documentary and cartographic evidence, encouraged the development of different and specialized methodologies. Though the extent of data on eighteenth century Louisbourg has proven to be an invaluable asset to the project over the past 30 years, it presented an almost insurmountable challenge to research staff in 1962 and 1963.[1]

The earlier commitment to high standards of research inspired by Senator John Stewart McLennan was reinforced by the first gen-

---

1   For a listing of manuscripts see Krause, Eric R., Master List of
     In-House Reports, Fortress of Louisbourg Archives, 1980.

eral consultant to the Louisbourg project, Ronald L. Way. He was one of few Canadians with broad experience in historic restorations, having directed the restoration of Fort Henry in Kingston, Ontario, Upper Canada Village in Morrisburg, Ontario and a number of other smaller historic properties for the Province of Ontario. His experience, however, was in the conduct and management of applied research programmes. This was a distinct advantage at this early stage of the Louisbourg project. It also helps to explain what was not researched by project staff throughout most of the 1960s, including important historical themes and subjects and a whole range of issues in social organization and behavior. Significant research by project historians on all of these subjects did not begin until the second decade of the research and development phase. The influence of these silences became evident in planning decisions and in the nature of many museum and historic site programmes.

Review of Way's research reports and memoranda from 1962 reveal clearly the sense of urgency that prevailed at that time in his new assignment at Louisbourg. The following quotation from the covering letter for a report on the fortifications of the King's Bastion is typical:

It had been my intention to include in this report, a section relating to the Chateau St. Louis for the information of the archaeologist. Unfortunately, time did not permit this since some of the most important documentary material did not arrive from Paris until a few days ago. I have recommended to Mr. Thorpe [Senior Historian for the project] that he should endeavour to produce immediately a report on the Chateau, to be followed by a similar dissertation on the subject of the Grand Battery.[2]

---

2   Way to Coleman, April 30, 1962, pp. 1-2, contained in Ms. Hf-7, Fortress of Louisbourg Archives.

The term Chateau St. Louis referred to a substantial building that had stood in the gorge of the King's Bastion, containing barracks for approximately 500 soldiers, the Governor's apartments, the garrison chapel, military offices and prison, and quarters for the chief financial officer for the colony. (The name Chateau St. Louis is no longer in use as it does not appear in original plans and documents referring to Louisbourg, but the building was the highest priority in the early development phase, which may explain why project staff contrived a suitably imposing name). The Royal Battery was also a high priority, though for preservation only. The extensive battery, its barracks and fortifications were not reconstructed, but were partially excavated prior to construction of a modern concrete wall to protect the ruins from erosion by the sea. These and other pressing development priorities were being formulated as the initial research was undertaken.

Ronald Way was determined to make the best of this difficult situation. In what was clearly one of the most important and earliest statements of research philosophy for the Louisbourg project, a memorandum on research submitted to the Director of the National Parks Branch, he opened with an uncomplicated precept: "A comprehensive research programme in both history and archaeology is the only basis for an authentic restoration of Louisbourg." [3] Though he was committed to a thorough research programme, he was equally aware, as a management consultant to the project, of the need to tailor that research to development objectives:

> Both avenues of research must be coordinated to the demands of the restoration programme to which the Government is committed, namely the provision of employment in the Cape Breton area, the product of which will ultimately be a partial reconstruction of the Fortress of Louisbourg and the creation of a visitor attraction con-

3   Way to Coleman, March 6, 1962, p. 1, contained in Ms. HF-1,
     Memorandum on Research, Fortress of Louisbourg Archives.

tributing both to the education and the economic development of Nova Scotia.[4]

The memorandum recommended a historical research programme in two distinct phases: an emergency programme to provide
information required for the 1962 construction work and a "more
orderly long-term programme" to keep pace with restoration. The
"crash-action historical research" consisted primarily of detailed research and analysis of a limited number of key documents and plans
pertaining mainly to the structural features and architectural components of the King's Bastion, concurrent with an effort to acquire
additional archival material in France and Britain, and, to a lesser extent, the United States. The long-term research was originally
intended to be comprehensive, utilizing archival and secondary
sources to provide information for a full range of museum programmes.

As museum programmes were not yet planned in any detail, historical research was concentrated on buildings and fortifications
until sufficient progress could be made in gathering source material
to allow informed decisions on research and development beyond
the King's Bastion and on subjects other than structural history.

King's Bastion Research Programme

Historical research on the King's Bastion was focused, specific, and
anything but academic. The historical reports and memoranda resulting from that research were concerned exclusively with the
structural details of buildings and fortification features. Research
and reporting methods were designed to meet specific development
objectives which could not be met by a standard historical narrative.
Some of these methodologies were neither commonly used nor fa-

---

4   Ibid., p. 4.

miliar to most university-trained historians. Their description here is intended to provide a case study in how professionally trained researchers from an established discipline, in this case history, can adapt to the requirements of a companion discipline, archaeology, as well as the disciplines of engineering and architecture.

The first change concerns the framework of questions developed by the historian after selection of the topic and completion of some preliminary research. Historians are normally accustomed to posing general questions as parameters for research and allowing detail and context to develop as research proceeds. For research on the King's Bastion specific questions were posed from the outset. How high and how thick was the parapet of the escarp wall? Were the steps to the barbette masonry or wood? How many and what size cannon were placed on the barbette and flanks of the bastion? What were the dimensions of the glacis slope? Thousands of such questions had to be answered. The impact of the eighteenth-century construction programme on the local economy or of the overall military policy of the English or New Englanders was not seen as being important at this point.

A second major change involved the chronological limits placed on the studies. Since Louisbourg had a brief history of French occupation (1713-1758 with a four-year interruption during English occupation from 1745-1749), there was already in place a set of chronological limits on studies of its history. Historical research on the King's Bastion was even more limited, focusing on the period from 1740-1758. Indeed, one of the most important reports included a recommendation to change the date to which the site would be reconstructed to the year 1745 from a mixture of dates spanning the history of the site up to 1758, including ruins from the 1760-61 period. Ultimately, that recommendation was followed because 1745 was a significant date in Louisbourg history and because it was simpler to reconstruct to one year than it would be to maintain a more evolutionary approach. This new strategy for reconstruction imposed a further and most unusual chronological limitation on historical research.

Other equally significant changes concerned the manner of presenting evidence and conclusions, as well as the type of source material consulted and subsequently included in reports. Few university-trained historians had experience in the close and detailed study of historical views, maps and plans, material specifications or construction technology. This was the province of geographers and architectural historians, but not academic historians in general. Research on the King's Bastion, however, had to be concerned almost exclusively with that type of source material, and this was reflected clearly in the reports. Invariably they included lists, tables and myriad illustrations, principally line drawings and copies of historical plans. In some reports text was kept to a minimum and there was little or no attempt to provide general context for the information presented.

The final major change in historical research methodology was in the manner of presenting research findings. Project briefs, memoranda, meeting minutes and formal and informal discussions with colleagues from other disciplines were favored over the traditional academic report. The practice developed in haste in 1962-63, but was retained as an acceptable and sometimes preferred method throughout the research and development phase of the project. The method was effective because it was quick and because the specific types of questions asked and the equally specific data consulted allowed researchers to think and write history in piecemeal fashion. These brief reports were no substitute for lengthy, more analytical research manuscripts, but they met the immediate requirements for information and collectively they provide an excellent resource for documenting the progress of research and development at the Louisbourg project. Because it was acceptable to report on research in this way the practice of writing down the basis for specific decisions on reconstruction features was established early in the project's development and formalized later in a committee system, leaving a large and important legacy in the project archives of minutes, letters, memoranda, project briefs and short reports. This important precedent was again set in the initial historical research on the King's

Bastion under the direction of Ronald Way, a practitioner of the art of applied research for many years previous.

Historical Records

The long-term historical research phase, as indicated above, could not be planned in detail until overall project planning (discussed in chapter two) advanced to a clearer definition of objectives. Historians not involved in studies of the King's Bastion soon became involved in a major effort to gather source material for later research. The extent of data was vast. Substantial financial resources and expertise were made available to find, copy and organize it, so the effort continued in earnest until 1966 and sporadically since that time.

Primary source material relating directly to Louisbourg can be divided into four broad categories: maps and plans, official correspondence, legal and commercial records and biographical and church records. The project archives also contains copies of royal proclamations and regulations of the Ministry of the Marine, which administered the French colonies, and of numerous journals from the first (1745) and second (1758) sieges. The number of private papers is insignificant compared to public records and there were no newspapers published at Louisbourg, though the completeness of court records more than compensates. In addition to primary sources, the project was able to acquire a variety of rare books published in the eighteenth century, including a complete edition of the Diderot Encyclopedia and other authoritative technical and specialized contemporary literature, all of which has been catalogued and in some cases indexed in the project library.

The following analysis of this data base emphasizes source material most frequently consulted by project historians and which has yielded the most useful and specific information for reconstruction, interpretation and education programmes. It does not attempt to assess the source material for general historical research or for its use in studies of New France or the French colonies in general. In other words, the analysis is restricted geographically and historiographically to Louisbourg, the capital of the colony of Ile Royale (Cape Breton and Prince Edward Island) and museologically to historical evidence that supported outdoor museum and historic site programmes.

Maps and Plans

The surviving collection of original and contemporary maps and plans pertaining to the colony of Ile Royale, was fortuitous. More than 500, located mainly in French and British archives, are extant, approximately 100 of which provide specific information on Louisbourg.[5] The town plans and views have been invaluable in the study of properties and structures within the area delineated for reconstruction. Many, perhaps 40 to 50, would be prized by any European or North American history museum and several of the watercolor plans, views and line drawings are works of art. Numerous examples could be provided, but three will serve the purposes of this analysis.

In 1731 the chief engineer at Louisbourg, Etienne Verrier and his son, referred to as Verrier fils, each drew watercolour views of the town from a ship in the harbour (see Figures 2 and 3). Wharves, streets, waterfront buildings and prominent public buildings were drawn in detail. Not surprisingly, close comparative study of documentary evidence and other plans has identified inaccuracies in the Verrier views, but they are excellent sources for the study of Louisbourg architecture in general and they provide accurate detail on

---

5   Map Collection, Fortress of Louisbourg Archives. There is a general inventory of holdings and file indices in various formats on hand in the archives. See also John Fortier, "The Fortress of Louisbourg and its Cartographic Evidence," *Bulletin of the Association for Preservation Technology*, Vol. 14, Nos. 1-2, 1972.

many structures and property features, especially on the waterfront where two entire town blocks and the waterfront facade of three others have been reconstructed. Where would project staff have been without these views? They have been copied countless times for research and design, in some cases half-inch sections of the original blown up photographically to 20 times their size for detailed analysis. The two views and several of the best overall property plans became the starting point for studies of Louisbourg buildings and fortifications and are invaluable for a visual conceptualization of the original harbour and town.

The second example of valuable cartographic evidence is a 1734 property plan drawn to finalize the results of Francois Vallee's official survey. In addition to delineating all properties in the town, the plan identifies each in a number and letter system that had been adopted early by the project staff to designate planned and already reconstructed properties and buildings. In North American terms it is an outstanding source for the study of eighteenth century town planning and it is one of the best contemporary indications of just how European Louisbourg was in concept and design. To the project historians and archaeologists it was one of the basic steps in developing an accurate orientation to the colonial town. Full-scale reproductions of the 1734 plan have been measured, overlaid with structures and property features and generally scrutinized and re-drawn in numerous reports and reconstruction drawings.

The third example is a 1768 British plan of the town accompanied by a detailed, written survey of all buildings (the fortifications had been demolished by the British in 1760). The plan is useful in the study of town occupancy and architectural evolution and in identifying New England and British structures that had replaced or altered original French structures. The written survey, in conjunction with the plan, is invaluable in its reference to pre-1745 features, as it serves to confirm or deny several important hypotheses about original construction and subsequent alterations, particularly for private properties that are not nearly as well documented as public buildings.

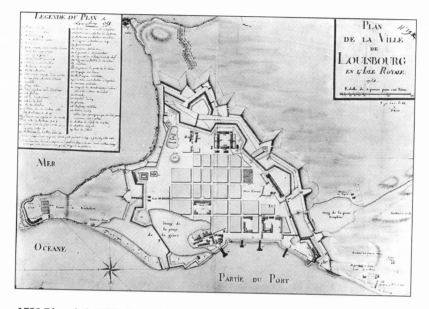

1758 Plan de la Ville de Louisbourg en l'Isle Royale. This plan shows the waterfront and the strenghthened fortifications as they appeared in 1758 during the second siege of Louisbourg. Source: France, BIBLIOTHEQUE NATIONALE, SERVICE TECHNIQUE DU GENIE.

In a typical research assignment these and other key plans and views (see Figure 4 for a typical example from 1731) would be rigorously compared to the remaining cartographic collection and subjected to all possible scrutiny from documentary evidence before conclusions could be drawn and contradictions resolved. There was an element of educated guesswork and outright conjecture in the progression from original research to final design drawings for reconstructed buildings and features, but the extent of cartographic evidence gathered early in the project's research effort has allowed a high degree of accuracy for the reconstruction of public buildings and a solid base for comparative study of many private properties, which, in turn, has led to a level of historical precision in the reconstruction of private buildings and features.

On a methodological level it is important to point out that all research and design disciplines used the collection of historical maps

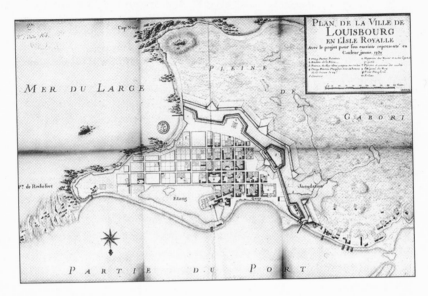

Figure 3: *1730 Plan de la Ville de Louisbourg.* This plan shows the nearly completed trace of the landward fortifications, progress made in the development of town blocks as well as scattered fishing properties along the shoreline outside the Dauphin Demi-Bastion. Source: ARCHIVES DE LA FRANCE D'OUTRE MER, DEPOT DES FORTIFICATION DES COLONIES.

and plans extensively. The project archaeologists, architects, and engineers were as familiar with the important maps and plans as historians and on a technical level they relied even more on the specific detail the collection could provide.

Official Correspondence

The Louisbourg archives contains copies of nearly one million pages of primary documentation on Ile Royale. The evidence has survived because Louisbourg was a colonial capital of international interest and historical significance and because France and England were sufficiently advanced culturally and institutionally by the middle of the eighteenth century to have established highly sophisticated archival procedures and resources. The legacy for the Louisbourg project has been a documentary record of remarkable proportions and rare completeness by North American standards. Research on this resource combined with research by archaeologists on an artifactual yield of equally remarkable richness, has produced an historical record of great importance in the study of colonial North America.

The official correspondence contained in several archival series illuminates virtually all aspects of colonial affairs.[6] Of particular importance in the early years of research were the many progress reports and detailed building specifications for the construction of fortifications and public buildings, usually submitted to the Minister of the Marine by the chief engineer at Louisbourg. These were essential to colaborate structural data, particularly proposals, that appeared on historical plans, elevations and profiles and they were routinely consulted by project archaeologists prior to excavation of properties. Construction detail confirmed by archaeological excavation would, of course, form the basis for reconstruction design. These documents were equally important in filling in gaps in construction detail left after analysis of archaeological data and preparation of as-found drawings, particularly in specifications for construction materials. Knowledge gained in the use of these sources for research, design and reconstruction of public buildings was later applied to the work on private buildings, for which there was a relative paucity of reliable historical evidence.

In addition to documenting colonial architecture and construction technology, the official correspondence provided a wealth of information on financial affairs, promotions and conflicts in command within the garrison, administrative practices and procedures, political and social structure, as well as a vast and fascinating amount

---

6   Paul Rose, Guide to the Louisbourg Archives: A Preliminary
      Inventory of Holdings, Ms. on file, Fortress of Louisbourg, 1972;
      Krause, E. and Cameron, M., The Fortress of Louisbourg General
      Inventory of Archival Holdings, Ms. on file, Fortress of Louisbourg,
      1981.

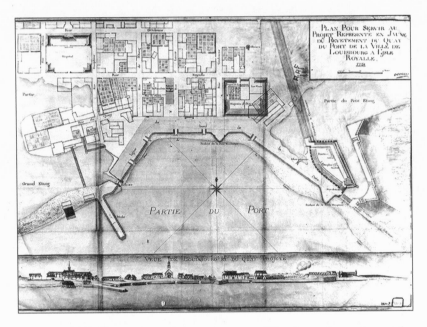

Figure 4: 1731 ***Plan pour servir au represente en View jaune du revetement du Quay du Port de la ville de Louisbourg. Vue de Louisbourg et du Quay projete.*** This plan and its accompanying view, drawn by the Chief Engineer of the colony, Etienne Verrier, shows in detail the buildings and town blocks along the waterfront as well as the fortifications along the shoreline. It has provided valuable information for many of the properties that have been reconstructed at Louisbourg. Source: France, BIBLIOTHEQUE NATIONALE.

of biographical detail on the people of colonial Louisbourg. The records have been used for studies of colonial policy and bureaucracy to a level of detail not normally available for colonial towns in North America. For example, a 1742 document provides a comprehensive list of stores contained in the King's storehouse which has been studied closely in attempts to furnish the reconstructed structure and to explain its role in the provisioning of the garrison and town. The same document contains information on the King's armory which has permitted the development of detailed designs for armory furniture and furnishings.[7] The official correspondence also reveals that the official declaration of war in 1744 reached Louisbourg weeks before New England was aware of the conflict, allowing the Louis-bourg military to launch a surprise attack on English possessions on mainland Nova Scotia.[8] Details of the expedition, which were chron-icled in the official correspondence, reveal important and specific information about the colonial town in the spring and summer of 1744, allowing a more accurate portrayal of the site in the reconstruc-tion and costumed animation programmes. For example, Captain Michel DeGannes, whose house on Block 17 has been recon-structed, was a member of the 1744 expedition. The present military animation programme at Louisbourg includes full interpretation of that property in 1744, including the fact of DeGannes' absence. There are numerous instances where such specific information about people and events has allowed a more accurate reconstruction and portrayal of the site, as well as a cumulative insight into the lives of many Louisbourg occupants and how their history can be presented to the public.

Legal and Commercial Records

For social history and material culture studies and, to a lesser extent, architectural history, the legal and commercial records are also vital to an authentic portrayal of eighteenth century Louisbourg. Having no recourse to elected representatives, the people of Louisbourg de-pended heavily on the colonial courts to redress grievances and settle disputes, as well as to legalize the acquisition and disposal of proper-ties and estates. The surviving records are meticulous and remarkably

---

7   Archives Nationales, Archives des Colonies, (hereafter cited as A.N., Colonies), C11B, Vol. 24, fols, 232-72, Balance des Magazins dy Roy 1742.

8   A.N., Colonies, B, Vol. 78, fol. 386, Maurepas to Bigot, 3 March, 1744.

complete, with just several years missing, from the early 1720s to 1758.[9]

Estate inventories provide the best example of how court records can be used for a variety of outdoor museum and historic site purposes. Most of the estate inventories provide a complete listing of the contents of the household of the deceased, the incompleteness of some inventories resulting from omission of goods not belonging to the estate but which may have been contained in the house as the possessions of another occupant. Consequently the inventories often provide a precise and in some cases complete furnishings plan for reconstructed houses.

The existence of estate inventories dated prior to 1745 for buildings within the planned area of the reconstruction provided the basis in later project planning for decisions on which buildings would be furnished to the period and which were designated to contain modern exhibits or services.[10] For example, the governor's apartment in the King's Bastion barracks is furnished according to the 1744 inventory of the estate of Governor Jean Baptiste DuQuesnel who died in October of that year, while the Julien Auger dit Grandchamp Inn and House on Block 2 has been furnished according to an estate inventory of 1741.[11] Additional research and analysis has often been required, for example, when an inventory had been taken during the winter for a house designated by the project planners to be furnished and interpreted to the summer of 1744 (the focus for interpretation

---

9   Archives de la France d'Outre Mer (hereafter cited as A.F.O.), G2, Registers of the clerk of the Superior Council of Louisbourg and G3, Notaries of Ile Royale 1727-1758.

10 John Lunn et al, "Interpretive Prospectus," Ms. on file, Fortress of Louisbourg, April 1972, pp. 11-14.

11 A.F.O., G2, Vol. 199, dossier 182, Inventaire de la succession de DuQuesnel, 22 Octobre 1744; and Vol. 197- 2, dossier 142, Inventaire de la succession de Grandchamp, 1741.

of the site), but the inventories provide in all cases an excellent starting point for curatorial efforts.

With more than 180 Isle Royale inventories available for study, it is possible to consult at least several inventories for almost any socio-economic group, providing an accurate knowledge base for the study of the material culture of colonial Louisbourg. In overall terms, the inventories reveal material culture patterns, such as the use of New England furniture and the common use of pewter and earthenware. Thousands of objects are listed and, in some cases, fully described in the inventories which have been used extensively in developing guidelines for the acquisition of furniture and furnishings for the reconstruction project.

Estate inventories also provide architectural information, especially those where the route taken by court officials through the house is described in the preamble to the actual inventory. Floor plans and room use for some reconstructed buildings have been based on evidence extrapolated from estate inventories, such as determining the approximate size of a room on the basis of what it contained or the functions it served.

Many of the inventories are accompanied by detailed reports on the sale of effects, allowing comparisons of evaluations in the inventory with the prices for which the objects actually sold in the sale. The tastes and living standards of Louisbourg residents can be determined or inferred, while social routine and lifestyle information can sometimes be gleaned from studying clothing inventories. A surprisingly few Louisbourg inventories list books, evidence which can support conclusions on levels of literacy, but also provide curatorial guidelines on when and where books should be on display. Bulk food lists in inventories provide clues on diet and storage conditions, which can be very useful in planning living history activities for some reconstructed historic properties.

Accounts of auction procedures in sale documents have allowed the scripting of scenarios for the re-enactment of auctions in the costumed animation programme, and they have provided much of the information base for an important sequence in a documentary film about life in the colonial town.[12] Finally, some inventories identifying relatives and associates can provide leads to other source material that may supplement biographical information, particularly on entrepreneurs whose properties include storehouses and for officers who were involved in commercial activities; in other words, most of the upper class.[13]

Estate inventories are generally more precise than surviving records of commercial and private transactions between companies and individuals. Nevertheless, the many contracts, sales agreements and recorded verbal testimonies in Louisbourg court records are essential and at times surprisingly specific in the study of such a commercially oriented capital. Virtually everyone in Louisbourg society, including military personnel up to the highest levels, was involved in some form of business or commercial activity, so these records can reflect the prevailing social mentality and daily routine of many of its inhabitants and visitors.[14]

Understanding these historical figures individually and collectively can be painstaking because of the extent of data. In the late

---

12　The Parks Canada film was produced at Louisbourg in 1979. Auction demonstrations have been a regular feature of the costumed animation programme during July and August.

13　This approach was used in the furnishing of the Rodrigue storehouse, for which there is no estate inventory. Other sources, however, indicate the commodities traded by Michel Rodrigue, his father and other business associates (see Christopher Moore, "The Maritime Economy of Isle Royale," *Canada, An Historical Magazine*, Vol. 1, No. 4, June 1974, pp. 41-42). There is also an estate inventory for two Louisbourg business partners involved in trading activity similar to Rodrigue's (see A.F.O., G2, Vol. 2045, folio 103, Inventaire des Solignac et Cabbarus), which provides a further basis for furnishing the Rodrigue storehouse.

14　Robert J. Morgan and Terrence D. MacLean, "Social Structure and Life in Louisbourg," *Canada, An Historical Magazine*, Vol. 1, No.4, June 1974, pp. 68-70.

1960s and early 1970s the court records in three important archival series were exhaustively indexed and described in finding aids as a preliminary step in the preparation of a comprehensive Domestic Architecture File. Other series from the official correspondence were included in this major effort to isolate information on buildings and property features. The resulting card file had serious flaws, which deserve analysis here primarily for methodological reasons, but the main point to be made in this description of the historical data base is that too much information was available to be researched in its entirety by each historian.

Research shortcuts had to be developed and systematic methods had to be deployed early to ensure cooperation among research colleagues in various disciplines, research assistants and clerical staff and later with operations staff as museum programmes were opened to the public. Sometimes the methods were efficient but wrong. The problems with the Domestic Architecture File can be reduced to two major shortcomings: one pertaining to its basic purpose, the other to research methods. There is a fundamental precept in good historical research that there is no substitute for consulting the original document. Researchers should seek to get that document or an exact, verifiable copy of it and then extract the information required to meet general or specific research objectives. The purpose of the Domestic Architecture File at Louisbourg was to transcribe and in many cases summarize the documents on file cards as a substitute for consulting archival copies of the originals. Omissions were inevitable, particularly in a research programme where objectives were evolving as the project planning process was refined, so most historians merely used the file as a finding aid which barely supplemented the existing finding aids. All important details had to be checked in the original, so it became apparent in anything but preliminary research that the file was no more than an overly complicated finding aid.

Concerning the methods used to establish the file, principally the decision to use unqualified research assistants and clerical staff to transcribe and in some cases locate the documents, standards for accuracy were too often compromised. Thorough checking against originals by experienced professional staff could not be included in the process — they were too busy producing reports — and many inaccuracies resulted. To avoid the consequence of including these inaccuracies in reconstruction design, professional research staff eventually had to routinely consult archival copies of the original documents to ensure that design staff were not applying incomplete or inaccurate versions in their work.

The efforts to complete the final stages of the file employed people and the effort can only be justified on that basis. But much effort was misapplied in the process. The risk of unnecessarily increasing the level of historical inaccuracy in reconstruction research and design existed if a less than competent research staff used the file. This brings the design and execution of this particular research initiative into serious question. It should have been designed as a finding aid for the exclusive use of qualified historians and archaeologists. Fortunately, when the file was in use during the research and development phase the project employed a well qualified, professionally trained research staff and attempts were made to correct the most serious deficiencies, but any museum or historic site without such research capability could easily compromise fundamentally important standards by failing to properly design and use its research files.

In this and other case studies used the difficulty of balancing socio-economic objectives with cultural or heritage preservation objectives will be analyzed. These case studies provide a manifestation of the extent to which Louisbourg as a museum and historic site was shaped by the economic imperatives inherent in the Canadian government's attempt to use the project to alleviate a chronic and vexatious problem in industrial Cape Breton — high unemployment. The application of this government policy was in this instance and in others at odds with acceptable professional standards.

The opportunities to organize, index, reorganize and otherwise exploit the archival data base at Louisbourg to provide employment have been a continuing feature of project planning and development. Most of the effort to organize and describe the contents of the

Louisbourg archives have contributed to a successful combination of archival source material and indexing, which ultimately resulted in an extensive, well organized and efficient project archives.

Occasionally contracts for private buildings are referred to in some detail in court records, but these references are rare and usually consist of brief descriptions of maintenance and repair work. Most of the historical information for reconstruction design of private buildings has been drawn from plans of the town and from a general knowledge of typical eighteenth-century French building techniques acquired by experienced professional and technical staff from all disciplines.

The many property disputes that had been recorded in court records have made a particularly large and very specific contribution to that state of knowledge. Such records are cited frequently in a series of architectural studies produced in the early 1970s and in a series of reports on the town blocks that were ultimately included in the reconstruction plan.[15] Louisbourg restructed contiguous buildings with a common wall on the property line. As in any urban community in Europe or North America, fences and outbuildings were also built along property lines. Inevitably legal disputes arose. A further impetus to this type of litigation was the building code, known as the Custom of Paris, which regulated in minute detail such matters as the height and distance of windows overlooking a neighbour's property. Records of these court proceedings make fascinating reading and provide insights into the transfer of French legal precedents and practices to the colonies, but more importantly for the early years of the Louisbourg project they often provided good descriptions of property and building features. Exploited rig-

---

15 B. Adams et al, Preliminary Architectural Studies, 31 articles
    organized in four volumes, Ms. on file, Fortress of Louisbourg,
    1971-1972. A series of 13 property reports were written between
    1969 and 1975. For a list of these reports see Krause, Eric R., Master
    List of In-House Reports, Fortress of Louisbourg Archives, 1980,
    section 8-HD.

orously by research and design staff, they frequently helped to precisely date features found during archaeological excavation that would otherwise have been subject to vague or altered stratigraphy and confused chronology, as happened on three separate occasions during research on substantial private buildings reconstructed on Block 4 properties.[16] This convergestorical and archaeological evidence in a precise and deliberately managed interdisciplinary method prior to property design and reconstruction became standard practice in the first five years of the Louisbourg project, and remained in place throughout the research and development phase.

Criminal records have on occasion also yielded structural information on buildings, properties and their use. One of the best examples pertains to a Block 16 property, where a theft took place in 1732.[17] A detailed description of the house was given as part of the investigation of the robbery. Some structural information on outside property features was also given in court testimony, as an occupant of the house, Jean Mercier, discovered evidence of the robbery when he went into the yard at six in the morning to relieve himself. As valuable as such court records are for information on buildings and property features, their true value lies in what they reveal about people.

Records of crimes and disputes are among the most important sources for social history research because collectively they described the lifestyles and concerns of all classes of Louisbourg society. They have compensated for a lack of personal diaries and newspapers as they provide specific, interesting and accurate supporting and supplementary information for labels, scripts and narrative texts in exhibits, staff lectures, and guided tours. Research staff who have worked with substantial amounts of this material have tended to de-

---

16 Terrence D. MacLean, A History of Block 4, Louisbourg:
    1713-1768, *Manuscript Report No. 176*, Parks Canada, Ottawa, 1974,
    pp. 16, 18-26, 51-53.

17 Robert J. Morgan, A History of Block 16, Louisbourg: 1713-1768,
    Manuscript Report No. 176, Parks Canada, Ottawa, 1975, pp. 24, 28.

velop a curious intellectual intimacy with Louisbourg people. Their lives become familiar and believable because their testimony is on record. Historians normally have access to primary source material on the leading political, military and social figures of eighteenth century Europe and North America, but studying the lower classes in such a stratified society can be difficult, easily overlooked or at least highly subjective if the words and sentiments of the illiterate are not recorded.

Chronologically, demographically and geographically, Louisbourg was a compact society, yielding through court records an easily managed and egalitarian case study in comprehensive social history. For example, through research into court records an extensive and convincing profile of the life of a typical servant or black slave in an upper middle class home can be developed, which provides the basis for portrayal of such people in the park's costumed animation programme.

Biographical and Church Records

For military personnel, especially officers, and some of the equally prominent members of civilian society, biographical records exist to supplement court records in the study of these prominent social groups. The personal dossiers of all of the chief military engineers and many other officers have survived, usually in the form of documentation for promotions and retirements.[18] As with the main categories of military and official correspondence, these records expose many issues in colonial affairs and they illuminate friendships and rivalries among colonial leaders. Through study of all categories of evidence it becomes obvious that in most years of the French colony's history there was a constant struggle for authority and social standing between the military governor and the chief administrative

18   Archives des Colonies, Serie E, Dossiers Personnels, 1638-1791.

official, known as the commissaire-ordonnateur. So much is revealed about the authorities, public involvements and practices of these individuals that a relatively clear picture of their private households and personal daily lives begins to emerge. The grand residences and working quarters of both officials have been included in the reconstruction, two very large and complex buildings, parts of which have been interpreted to the public as they are presumed to have been in the summer of 1744 when the sickly Jean Baptiste Duquesnel was governor and the ambitious and autocratic Francois Bigot was financial commissary. As with some of the well documented public buildings reconstructed early in the project's research and development phase, there is very little guesswork in the historical information on these gentlemen as they were later presented to the public.

The same categories of official and military sources and court records, also provide reliable biographical information on the large group of merchants, mariners and officers at Louisbourg who were involved in trading operations, particularly when such records are supplemented by shipping registers and commodity lists. More important, however, than the sometimes fragmentary information on the ships and cargoes of individual entrepreneurs is the overall sense they convey of the maritime flavour of the community.[19] Without such records on the port of Louisbourg and the even more profuse records on the principal western and southwestern ports of France it would be easy and inaccurate to conceptualize Louisbourg merely as a military post where two important colonial battles were fought; a theme that dominated the Canadian historiography of Louisbourg and Isle Royale before the reconstruction project began.[20] Study of

---

19 Archives des Colonies, Serie F1A, Fonds des colonies; Serie F2A, Compagnie de commerce and Archives Charente- Maritime (La Rochelle), Registres et liasses, Louisbourg Admiralty Court.

20 There are several bibliographies on Louisbourg available in the project library. A graduate paper prepared at the University of Ottawa by Christopher Moore is probably the best. The bias toward military events is most evident in Francis Parkman, *Half Century of Conflict*, Boston, Little, Brown, 1892, Vol. 2.

the wealth of data on extensive private trade and the associated international cod fishery quickly leads to a more accurate perception of Louisbourg as a thriving Atlantic port fortified for economic and not strictly strategic reasons. This research has produced a change in thinking that has profoundly influenced the interpretation of Louisbourg to the public in recent years. It is important to emphasize here that the extent and significance of non-military records that have survived in French, British and even some North American repositories leads directly to this fundamental change in perception by historians and ultimately by the public.

Church records have also been invaluable for biography and social history in general. The parish records for all but the first nine years of the colony's existence have survived.[21] Their information goes beyond substantiating the importance of religion in Louisbourg society or revealing the beliefs, rituals and practices for births, weddings and funerals. Studies of kinship, social relations, literacy, sexuality and illegitimacy, infant mortality, occupation patterns, transience, the effects of climate, incidence of disease, and of prevailing medical practices are supported by statistics and correlative analysis of population patterns from parish records. These records have been thoroughly indexed because they are the starting point for the biographical study of individuals and families within the reconstructed area. Two examples, one specific and one general, indicate the importance of these sources for museum and historic site programmes.

The first example concerns two Louisbourg families related by marriage, the Lartigues and the Rodrigues. Joseph Lartigue was a merchant and judge and one of the first civilians appointed to the governing council of the colony, the Superior Council. Michel Rodrigue, a merchant at Louisbourg, married one of Lartigue's daughters. Both Lartigue and Rodrigue had large, extended families and originally lived in houses within what was later to become the reconstruction area of the Louisbourg project. By 1744 Lartigue's family num-

---

21 A.F.O., Serie G1, Registres de l'etat civil, recensements et divers
    documents, 1721-1784.

bered 19, while Rodrigue's totaled at least 12.[22] The precise size of each house is known from historical and archaeological evidence and in Lartigue's case it is known that court sessions were regularly held at his residence on the Louisbourg waterfront. Crowded conditions definitely prevailed in both residences, which suggests full use of all space, probably temporary partition walls, collapsible furniture and limited storage. These have been important considerations in the reconstruction and interpretation of both properties.

The second and more general example of information derived from church records is the pattern of intermarriage between officers and wealthy merchant families. Though most apparent in the parish records, the pattern is also clear from court records and official correspondence. More is known about the senior officers and in a general sense all officers, because of the extent of military records, allowing the reconstructed homes of the military to serve as a reference point for the material culture and lifestyle of the equivalent civilian elite. This pattern can also suggest appropriate social encounters between civilian and military personnel that can be depicted in exhibits, publications, and in animation scenarios to bring out the true nature of Louisbourg society. In other words, it serves to reinforce the blend of military and civilian influences in Louisbourg society and to discredit any contention that one group either dominated or excluded the other.

Contemporary Published Sources

The above categories of primary source material provide the principal basis for the reconstruction and interpretation of historic Louis-

---

22 Kenneth Donovan, "Communities and Families: Family Life and Living Conditions in Eighteenth Century Louisbourg," *Material History Bulletin, No. 15*, Ottawa, National Museum of Man, 1979, pp. 39-40.

bourg to the public. Published sources have also been invaluable, especially contemporary books, treatises, letters and journals that have been grouped in what the project archives refers to as the rare book collection.[23] Appropriately, the first entry in the collection catalogue is the Diderot "Encyclopedie, ou Dictionnaire raissone des science, des arts et des metiers, par une societe de gens des lettres." It has, if anything, been over-utilized by project staff because it contains a wealth of technical information that is relevant only in a general sense to eighteenth century Louisbourg. As a substitute for original sources, it can be misleading, but as a general guide to the science, technologies and crafts of the eighteenth century it is exceptionally rewarding. Used as a supplement to the primary historical documentation and archaeological evidence it is an invaluable source of information for reconstruction design. Designs of building features and furnishings have sometimes been based directly on Diderot data when original Louisbourg sources have not been available. It has been the standard reference work for all technical research in architecture, material culture, and crafts at the Louisbourg project.[24]

Numerous additional entries in the rare book collection provide references to practices in military architecture and engineering, in French cuisine and etiquette, and to many military procedures and regulations. Published military codes and treatises have been particularly useful in the study of garrison routine and inherent attempts to control the civilian population.[25] Several acquisitions

---

23 Krause, Eric R., A List of Rare Books, September 1977, Ms. on file, Fortress of Louisbourg.

24 Denis Diderot, Encyclopedie . . . lettres, Paris, Briasson, Plates (11 volumes) 1762-72; Text (17 volumes) 1751-65.

25 Three examples will suffice: *Blondel, Cours d'architecture* . . . , Paris, Desait, 1771; Menon, *La Cuisiniere bourgeoise* . . . , Bruxelles, 1772; *Ordonnance du Roy sur l'exercise de l'infanterie*, Paris, 1755. There are approximately 150 titles in the collection.

would be prized by museums; for example, the handwritten manuscript prepared circa 1737 to document Vauban's "Traite de fortifications" in three volumes, complete with watercoloured plans, profiles, and drawings.[26] It was purchased for exhibition and not for research purposes, since there are many reliable published works on the Vauban system of fortification and also a wealth of primary and published cartographic and documentary evidence on the adaptation of the bastioned trace. Many other eighteenth century books have also been purchased exclusively for display in furnished homes and offices within the reconstruction area, but these are generally of limited value for research purposes.

Two contemporary written accounts of sojourns in Louisbourg were published: Thomas Pichon's written in 1758 and published in 1760, and an anonymous "Letter of an Inhabitant" written in 1745 and published with a translation in 1897.[27] Pichon's book is generally accurate, but contains nothing new in its descriptions of Louisbourg and the rest of Ile Royale. Its value lies in its analysis of personalities and their reaction to events, not in the author's rather subjective reports on those events, for Pichon was a spy for the English. It is a good source, nevertheless, to convey the wartime mentality of Louisbourg people. Underlying Pichon's version of events is an indication of how the lives of ordinary people are affected by the attitudes and decisions of their leaders.

The anonymous letter is more specific chronologically, focusing on Louisbourg in 1745, and for that reason even more useful to the Louisbourg project than Pichon's work in describing the impact of a colonial war on a mid-eighteenth century community. Both ac-

---

26 Sebastian Le Preste de Vauban, *Traite de Fortification*, Paris, 1737.

27 Thomas Pichon, *Genuine Letters and Memoirs, Relating to the Natural, Civil and Commercial History of the Islands of Cape Breton and Saint John*. London. J. Nourse. 1760; George M. Wrong, ed., *Louisbourg in 1745: The Anonymous Lettre D'un Habitant de Louisbourg*, containing a narrative *by* an eye-witness of the siege in 1745. Toronto. Warwick Bro's and Rutter.1897.

counts must be used in conjunction with primary source material, but the flesh they add to official accounts helps to start the process of inquiry on what the people of Louisbourg were thinking about, their ambitions and, in these two accounts, their apprehensions.

Eighteenth century French and English literature provides some of the best sources to support an analysis of the likely behavior and psychology of Louisbourg people and how they lived. The project library has not confined its holdings to academic and technical literature. In acquiring source material the purchasing policy was set with wider parameters. From Rousseau and Voltaire on politics to Montesquieu, Marivaux and Fielding on society, the benefits to be gained from reading contemporary scholarship and fictional novels were recognized. Over the past three decades the Louisbourg project, as with any well financed and professionally directed museum, has accumulated as much relevant secondary source material as staff could locate, and this published literature has been in regular use since the research staff, archives and library were finally moved to Louisbourg in their entirety in 1968.

The extensive effort to gather source material, the teamwork developed in the use of historical evidence, and the combined study of literary and non-literary source material, were the most important characteristics of the first 20 years of historical research by Louisbourg staff. It has made a major contribution to the development of Canada's most ambitious outdoor museum and historic site.

CHAPTER 2
Planning & the Role of Research

Earlier it was indicated that a long-term historical research programme could not be planned in detail "until overall project planning advanced to a clearer definition of objectives to which research could respond."[1] To understand the Louisbourg research and development process it is necessary to investigate that planning process, including the contributions made by research staff and the mechanisms developed to coordinate the process within the National Parks Branch (later known as Parks Canada). To properly explain and evaluate this process it is also necessary to outline the financial context for work at Louisbourg from 1961 to 1964.

Financial Context

On March 3, 1961 three proposals were submitted to the Cabinet of the Federal Government of Canada in Ottawa for the restoration of the Fortress, "roughly estimated to cost six, twelve and eighteen mil-

---

1   See above, p. 19.

lion dollars respectively." The Cabinet approved a "crash" programme of one million dollars to be spent by March 31, 1962.[2]

Construction started on July 1, 1961, just two weeks after the
details of a major restoration project at Louisbourg were announced
in the House of Commons. The Cabinet also approved an additional twelve million dollars over a period of "about twelve years".
Capital expenditures (excludes operating and maintenance costs) of
one and a half million dollars were planned for each fiscal year up to
and including 1965-66, with $1,670,000 allotted for 1966-67. The
Cabinet further stipulated that "a fairly spectacular showing" must be
made by July 1, 1967, "the date of Canada's centennial as a nation."

This budget and its inherent annual schedule immediately placed
the Louisbourg project into the mainstream of major growth in
Canada's cultural institutions in the years preceding and following
centennial celebrations in 1967. The spectacular showing was to
coincide with the World's Fair at Montreal, Expo '67, which stimulated museum growth in Canada.[3] Canada's maturity as a nation of
three peoples, English, French, and native Indian was often emphasized by Progressive Conservative and Liberal Governments and
their bureaucrats throughout this period. The Louisbourg project
benefited financially from this political and social climate and from
the continuing difficulties in the Cape Breton economy, but the

---

2   Excerpts from Minister's Handbook, September 1963, in Fortress of
    Louisbourg Archives, project file 53-1, special progress report,
    unpaged.

3   Crowdis, Donald K. "Development of Canadian Museums",
    Conference Proceedings for 2001: The Museum and the Canadian Public,
    Ottawa, Canadian Museums Association, 1977; and Key, A. *Beyond
    Four Walls: The Origins and Development of Canadian Museums*,
    Toronto, McClelland and Stewart, 1973; Alexander, Edward P.,
    Museums in Motion, Nashville, American Association for State and
    Local History, 1979; and Burcaw, G. Ellis, *Introduction to Museum
    Work*, Nashville, American Association for State and Local History,
    1975.

funds were approved before an acceptable planning process for research and development was even attempted.

Financial allotments between 1961 and 1967 increased steadily with the addition of winter works projects and a growing operating and maintenance budget. This pattern continued after the official opening of the King's Bastion to the public in 1967. A recent review of total expenditures, capital and operating and maintenance on the project from 1961-1985 produced an overall estimate of approximately $75,000,000. The principle points to be made here are that the project was already a well funded, complex reconstruction by 1964 and that it remained so throughout the period of research and development at Louisbourg, a status which has continued since that time. The current overall annual budget at the Fortress of Louisbourg National Historic Site is approximately six million dollars. Employment figures further illustrate the rapid growth and major scope of the project in its early years.

Table I
EMPLOYMENT FIGURES 1961-1964,
(Taken From Report on Progress, June 19, 1964, Appendix F)

Date	Total Strength
July 15, 1961	31
September 15, 1961	98
December 13, 1961	175
March 30, 1962	177
May, 1962	216
June, 1963	240
July 15, 1964	246

Research and Planning

Serious scheduling problems began to develop early, particularly in the provision of research data to engineering and architectural design staff. These problems persisted throughout the first decade of research and reconstruction, but they were particularly acute in the early and mid 1960s when the research staffs worked in separate locations; Archaeological research took place in Louisbourg and historical research in Ottawa. The engineering and architecture staff were also dispersed — though not to the same extent — because all reconstruction drawings had to be approved by the National Parks Branch in Ottawa after they had been reviewed by the General Consultant, Ronald Way. He spent most of his time in Ontario after the project staff became established in Louisbourg and Ottawa in 1962 and 1963. Way also served as Research Director during this period and was the principal focus of responsibility in attempts to coordinate research and design. Everyone, especially the large professional staff in disciplines of archaeology, architecture, engineering and historical research, was under pressure to produce significant results at Louisbourg because the project had already attained a high profile within the National Parks Branch and within the Canadian public.

On the local level the project was already a major employer and tourist attraction with economic and cultural potential that was conspicuously high. The challenge to coordinate the various professional disciplines and to apply their results in construction activity was apparent and vexing. By 1963 the problem became serious enough to require a special report on the progress of the reconstruction. The report and the exchange of correspondence preceding it consistently cited research delays as a serious problem. The investigation effort was carried out primarily by engineers in senior positions at Louisbourg, in consultation with their disciplinary counterparts in the Halifax.

There was an underlying assumption on the part of senior managers, decision makers and even policy analysts in the Parks Branch that engineers could schedule other staff. This assumption exacerbated what would have been a serious problem anyway, as engineers and their staff developed work schedules, charts, internal progress reports and budget submissions almost in isolation and abstraction, with no knowledge of historical and archaeological method and little regard for contingency planning outside their own discipline. The early correspondence reveals that the project engineers delayed the point at which a full recognition and appreciation of the affinity of disciplines and occupational groups could develop.

The special progress report was initially requested on a priority basis in September 1963, by the Director of the National Parks Branch, J.R.B. Coleman.[4] In November instructions were issued by the Project Manager, A.D. Perry, to project staff to report only on work completed.[5] By this time consultants and contractors were very much involved in the reconstruction, however, which probably explains why an effort was made to explain away the report as "not completed or forwarded to Ottawa", because knowledge of scheduling problems was now widespread and beyond the damage control strategy of the project engineers.[6] The request for a formal progress report was further reinforced in March, 1964 by the Cabinet Minister responsible for the National Parks Branch, Arthur Laing. In a memorandum from Laing's executive assistant to the Deputy Minister, E.A. Cote, the financial context was emphasized: "The Minister would like to have an up-to-date report on progress in Louisbourg with particular emphasis on whether we are getting full value for the money being spent."[7] Cote issued specific instructions to park staff to utilize the General Consultant to the project, Ronald Way.[8]

---

4   Coleman to Perry, Sept. 9, 1963, in Fortress of Louisbourg Archives, project file 53-1, special project report, unpaged.

5   Ibid., Perry to Lunn, Thorpe, Vachon, Nov. 5, 1963.

6   Ibid., handwritten notation on memorandum, Perry to Lunn, Thorpe, Vachon, n.d.

7   Ibid., Gibson to Cote, March 4, 1964.

Ottawa officials were concerned that the Louisbourg project, already a major factor in National Parks Branch commitments to expenditures and staff, was extending beyond their expectations and beyond their parameters for the development of individual historic parks and sites in the wider parks system.

The resulting and official progress report was both a chronicle of problems encountered and a record of impressive accomplishments from 1961-64.[9] The historical research component of the report addressed the obvious problem of having too little time to conduct general studies of the fortress area and was defensive about research results described as "by-products to assist certain aspects of restoration." Included in the report of work completed, however, was the copying, accessioning, classification and cataloguing of the historical maps and plans; the most important archival source for the archaeological and reconstruction work. Historical research staff organized this collection for use by the other disciplines at Louisbourg and ultimately for use by interested members of the public. Organization of the maps and plans and the further gathering of documentary source material were the most important contributions that the historical research staff could make at this early stage to the collective process of initiating and sustaining a quality reconstruction over the long term. This early effort to study, analyze and interpret the available historical documentation for use by historians and by those trained in other disciplines constituted the first stage in a multi-disciplinary approach to reconstruction research and design, a sophisticated process that endured for more than two decades and was carried forward in the operational phase of the project. Edward Larabee, Senior Archaeologist at Louisbourg during most of the period covered in the progress report, wrote in a 1971 article on archaeological research at Louisbourg, 1961-65:

---

8   Ibid., Coleman to Way, copy to Perry, March 12, 1964.

9   Ibid., Report on Progress, with covering letter dated June 19, 1964, p.p. 1-24.

This was part of a larger research program in which we were trying to bring archaeological and historical studies into proper sequence. An ordered dialogue between the disciplines would present the evidence and draw the conclusions for an accurate reconstruction of the Citadel, and would record all the steps by which this reconstruction had been reached.[10]

"An ordered dialogue between the disciplines": an excellent phrase that sums up the essence of an informal planning and development process that was enlarged and improved after 1964. A formal committee system to facilitate the dialogue between the research disciplines and the closely allied disciplines of architecture and engineering as established and this action comprised a concerted attempt to give more weight to historical and archaeological evidence than to any one discipline's interpretation of that evidence.

One of the major conclusions of the 1964 progress report respecting research was that the staff had to be increased. Close study of the rationale for that conclusion reveals that the author, Ronald Way, was concerned about the capability of existing staff and the prospects for recruitment of additional staff, particularly in historical research. He referred to the "lack of capable staff" and to the failure of "numerous recruiting campaigns over the past two years . . . to yield acceptable candidates who [sic] would have suitable academic qualifications to undertake the work we require at Louisbourg."

The issue was cooperation, in the form of the "dialogue between disciplines" referred to by Larabee. By training and by disposition academic historians were accustomed to working on their own or with other historians, rarely with representatives of other disciplines. Way had long since forsaken university work. With long experience as a practitioner in the field of historic restoration he was used to

---

10 Edward McM. Larabee, "Archaeological Research at the Fortress of Louisbourg", *Occasional Papers in Archaeology and History No. 2*, passim.

working with a variety of technically oriented professionals and instinctively he knew the kind of detailed information they needed to get on with their job. Many historians did not appreciate this requirement. Most Canadian university history departments were not then interested in public or popular history and they largely ignored the entire historic preservation movement. Consequently many of their graduates were not prepared for the special demands of the Louisbourg project.

Ronald Way was not alone in expressing these concerns. In October, 1963 the Park Superintendent at Louisbourg, John Lunn, submitted a report on Interpretation at the Fortress of Louisbourg to the Project Manager, Dave Perry. It outlined an ambitious range of programmes, emphasizing the need for research input to implement them. "I am well aware that the major difficulty lies in the exceedingly complex analytical problems that face the Director of Research and his staff."[11] In a supplement to the report Lunn called for research on an urgent basis into such subjects as furniture, textiles, glass, pottery, ceramics and small metal work. He then offered this general comment: "I sometimes think that there is too great a tendency on this project to regard research as ancillary to what is thought of as an engineering matter."[12] He requested the addition of one historian to his staff as a key position in ensuring progress in the interpretive field. "For want of a better word, I have described him as an historian, but the position could perhaps be described with greater accuracy as a Researcher . . . his main function will be to do research in those areas that the Research section is clearly not ready to explore itself at this stage of the project."[13]

---

11 John Lunn, Interpretation — a Preliminary Report on the Fortress of Louisbourg National Historic Park, Ms.. on file, Fortress of Louisbourg, Oct. 23, 1963, p. 9.

12 Ibid., supplement to report of October 23, 1963, p. 1.

13 Ibid., p. 7.

Both Way and Lunn raised the issue of how the results of research were presented and utilized.[14] Already the project's development had reached the point where research contributions to other disciplines and to the planning process were more important than academic reports or scholarly articles in historical publications. By 1965, urgent demands for historical information began to come from these expanded interpretation programmes and increased reconstruction activity, adding to the pressure on the Ottawa research staff to produce specialized reports, to provide access to research collections and to contribute to long-range planning.[15] Once again Ronald Way was asked for a special report:

> Since research is the base for restoration, furnishings and interpretation, it is therefore, at present, impossible to adequately plan the reconstruction and interpretation developments and it is necessary that the Department be advised on this serious problem while at the same time giving our recommendations on how this can be improved.[16]

Research and Development

The document gave an overview of construction and interpretation projects delayed because of a lack of historical and archaeological information and sympathized with the claims by research staff that insufficient time was available and research must control the pace of the project. Related issues were raised such as the recruitment and

---

14 See above, chapter 1.

15 Lunn to Perry, Sept. 20, 1965, Fortress of Louisbourg Archives, project file 53-1.

16 Ibid., Perry to Way, Sept. 20, 1965.

training of research staff, how information was to be conveyed to engineering and architectural staff and the role of each discipline in the overall effort.[17] Two of its principal recommendations were eventually followed, which significantly altered both the pace and the nature of the research and reconstruction effort and ultimately the quality of its presentation to the public. Before they are discussed in detail, however, the Louisbourg project has to be placed in the broader context of the Parks Canada system in 1965.

Although the system was decentralized with its natural parks, canals, rivers and historic sites and monuments growing in every region of the country, a strong headquarters office in Ottawa exerted the determining influence on the establishment of new parks and sites and the preservation, growth and renewal of existing ones. The national museums by this time were firmly rooted in the capital city in another federal government department and national cultural agencies such as the Canada Council flourished in Ottawa with a highly centralized bureaucracy and increased funding. That pattern continued under Liberal governments during and after the 1967 centennial under Prime Ministers Lester Pearson and later Pierre Trudeau, who visited Louisbourg in 1971.[18] The decade between 1965 and 1975 was one of unprecedented expansion for national cultural agencies such as Parks Canada and Louisbourg was a significant part of that process. But the major policy decisions were made in Ottawa, particularly in the areas of research and planning.

Not surprisingly the Research Division of Parks Canada was located in Ottawa and worked closely with the other divisions of the Parks Branch. The regional office in Halifax, was largely administrative and only senior management participated in major decisions at this time, with no staff or major responsibilities in the functional ar-

---

17 Way to Perry, October 19, 1965, Fortress of Louisbourg Archives, Project File 53-3.

18 Cape Breton Post, August 2 and 3. 1971, as copied for scrapbook #4, Fortress of Louisbourg Archives.

eas such as research. Louisbourg, because of its size and scope after 1961 had its own historical research staff, but they were also located in Ottawa. Archaeological excavations in Louisbourg, for example, were closely integrated with the Research Division in Ottawa and source gathering by historians was directed by the Research Division and coordinated with the National Archives in Ottawa. Project staff and consultants such as Ronald Way traveled extensively and attempted to coordinate the disparate functions, but it was often a frustrating effort as the Way memorandum and other correspondence from this period reveals. The challenge was not just to bring "disciplines" together but to do so in an integrated functional and administrative setting while retaining central control in Ottawa.

Although experienced in the establishment and operation of large national parks such as Banff, Alberta and Cape Breton Highlands, Parks Canada had to face the Louisbourg problem largely as an experiment, and without sufficient time to plan in a methodical and sophisticated manner. The research and resource management efforts required for natural parks were very different from what needed to be applied to historical resources such as surviving buildings and archaeological remains. There were few successful models to follow in 1965. It was obvious that much had to be learned at Louisbourg for the benefit of the whole Canadian system.

The scheduling difficulties encountered in design and reconstruction activity at Louisbourg were resolved as more experienced engineering and architectural staff began to work cooperatively with research staff, but the conflicts to be resolved for the interpretation programmes at Louisbourg were even greater and would require a special effort, one that eventually became the model Canada lacked in such undertakings. Study of these efforts and their comparison with another major Parks Canada planning process a decade later for historic sites in Halifax reveal a pattern that reflects the gradual maturity of the system. In both cases people were brought together at the original site, not just in Ottawa headquarters, and remarkable progress was made. In the process Louisbourg became a training ground for the entire system of historic parks and sites in Canada and a testimony to the frustrations and ultimately the growth and maturity of the national preservation, interpretation and public history movement.

The immediate problem in 1965 was not interpretation planning or overall systems planning. The problem was getting research information to engineers and architects who could, in theory, use it in design and reconstruction. In his memorandum Ronald Way favoured handing the raw data to engineers and architects, and this passage needs to be quoted in full in order to reach an understanding of a later qualification that proved to be vital to the nature and progress of work at Louisbourg:

> My preference would be to feed the required information to engineers and architects in the form of annotated excerpts direct from the manuscript and archaeological sources. In the case of historical evidence, these direct references could be expeditiously assembled if we were to employ the system of transferring all information to cross-referenced note cards — the system which . . . the former Research Director agreed to use but which the Senior Historian did not approve and discarded.[19]

The issue inherent in this debate was methodological. Who was to consult and just as importantly who was to interpret the original source material? The historians and archaeologists were determined to protect their disciplinary prerogatives and were equally adamant that proper training and education were necessary in order to work competently with original source material. Both were reluctant to submit data to colleagues without being part of its analysis and its interpretation. Way qualified his recommendation by proposing that "a committee including the construction engineers, the architects and the researchers should meet to discuss and project the informa-

---

19 Way to Perry, October 19,1965, Fortress of Louisbourg Archives, Project File 53-3.

tion." The key element in this recommendation was the participation of research staff in the design process, later formalized as the Structural Design Committee, which eventually led to their participation in all phases of the design, reconstruction and interpretation activity for the project, including planning.

A second major recommendation in the memorandum concerned the location of the historians in Ottawa, which "can no longer be justified...their disassociation with the realities of the restoration has tended to encourage their predilection to a purely academic approach." Way strongly recommended the transfer of the research staff and relocation of the project archives and library to Louisbourg, which was done between 1966 and 1968, after his recommendations were approved by the Director of the National Parks Branch.[20] This brought together in one location the various disciplines working on the Louisbourg project and produced a "critical mass" that would benefit Louisbourg and Parks Canada in general in the years of expansion that followed.

Research staff were relocated at a time when the Louisbourg project was entering a different phase of development. Despite the many difficulties, significant progress had been made in design and reconstruction and major areas of the King's Bastion were open to the public, which increased interest in the reconstruction effort and focused attention on the need to interpret to the public even more of Louisbourg's history and its reconstruction. After 1965 Louisbourg staff were faced with simultaneously building and interpreting the historic site to increasing numbers of visitors for six months of the year, May to October, and to interested members of the museum and historic site community all year long. As Louisbourg achieved a higher profile in the museum and heritage preservation movement, encouraged by the promotional efforts of senior staff and the media impact of such a large undertaking, pressure increased to show results on a year by year basis and to justify expenditures within Parks

---

20 Malis to Cote, October 22, 1965, Fortress of Louisbourg Archives, project file 53-1, p.3-4.

Canada and to politicians, media and to the general public. As much as some staff wanted to work unfettered by these demands, they could not do so under the changed circumstances at the Louisbourg project without becoming isolated and ineffectual. This was particularly true for research staff, which was reflected in a very high turnover rate in the decade following relocation to Louisbourg.[21]

Archaeological and historical research had to adjust to these new requirements while continuing to provide information for the reconstruction of properties. Relocation to Louisbourg was an advantage for both the reconstruction effort and in the preparation of major displays on the process itself, because the source material and the people who knew it best were now available to the project's interpretation specialists as well as to the reconstruction staff. Two large and popular displays in the King's Bastion demonstrated the new opportunities presented by the relocation and by the gradual shift in emphasis in the research programme.

A display on the first floor of the barracks of the King's Bastion incorporated numerous archaeological artifacts to explain to the visiting public the basis for the reconstruction surrounding them. One of the principal display techniques was to place the artifact from the excavations in the background of a display case with a full-scale reproduction in the foreground. Representative artifacts were readily available from the research collections and reproductions of such objects as cut stones and building hardware were routinely made in Louisbourg shops for use in the reconstruction. Research that had been conducted for reconstruction design was applied directly, simply and effectively in this particular attempt to explain the extensive

21 John Lunn, Interpretation - a Preliminary Report on the Fortress of Louisbourg National Historic Park, Ms.. on file, Fortress of Louisbourg, Oct. 23, 1963, p. 9 : Lunn to Perry, Sept. 20, 1965, Fortress of Louisbourg Archives, project file 53-1. : Way to Perry, October 19,1965, Fortress of Louisbourg Archives, Project File 53-3. The turnover rate for professional staff in the decade 1965-1975 improved from a duration of approximately 18 months to more than three years.

Louisbourg construction activity to the public and to bring together all of the elements necessary for a successful display, especially the research collections and expert knowledge of them. Throughout the months from May to October visitors could see archaeological excavation underway at various locations within the reconstruction and many became as interested in the research and reconstruction process as they were in the original history of the fortress and town. Such displays were able to satisfy this curiosity without seriously disrupting research and reconstruction activity, but the necessity of interpreting Louisbourg's history and its reconstruction to the public was becoming a further distraction from pure and applied research and sustained, focused development.

Another display, the refurnished Governor's Apartment in the King's Bastion barracks, indicated the changing applications for historical research and the pressing need to plan interpretation activity. A decision was made to furnish the apartment to the year 1744, just prior to the first siege and bombardment. The Louisbourg Governor, Jean Baptiste DuQuesnel, died in October of that year and a detailed estate inventory provided the basis for furnishing the apartment. The period display was one of the first attempts to interpret Louisbourg interiors, proving to be just as complicated as exterior reconstruction and requiring a similar array of specialized information and staff. It was also one of the first displays to fit into an overall scheme for the interpretation of the site and as such it set the standards for the planning and development of properties elsewhere.

Although the building was well documented and historical and archaeological research on exterior and interior features was extensive, not all questions with respect to interior partitions, room location and use could be answered definitively with the evidence available. As with any building interior, arrangements evolved through time and even the choice of a specific date and association with one person's household, however well documented, did not ensure precise information on the many details to be included in an authentic representation of the apartment. Just as accuracy was paramount in the reconstruction of building exteriors, so too was authenticity in the furnishing and portrayal of interiors; again scheduling became critical. The public could not be left to wait indefinitely while research proceeded and curators acquired collections. Additional questions such as traffic flow, visitor safety, security and appropriateness of new interpretation media had to be addressed before designers and other interpretation specialists could begin their work.

In 1963 the Park Superintendent, John Lunn, had requested the addition of an historian to his staff in Louisbourg.[22] At that time the research staff as well as the engineering, design and construction staff reported to a Project Manager and worked in various locations, but they were not directly responsible to the Park Superintendent who was in charge of all other operations at Louisbourg, including interpretation, so the request was reasonable in that context. It also underlined the need to bolster the interpretation effort. The final relocation of the research staff, archives, library and project research files to Louisbourg and the subsequent consolidation of all Louisbourg staff under the Park Superintendent eliminated the need for a separate research effort, and also made more expertise and resources available for new interpretation projects.

Progress at Louisbourg between 1965 and 1975 was largely due to his leadership and the methods chosen to get the job done. The Governor's Apartment was a microcosm of how he operated.

Among the keys to Lunn's success were his close personal involvement in virtually every facet of the Louisbourg project and the encouragement he gave to all staff, not just archaeologists and historians, to conduct research and become generally informed about Louisbourg's history. The requirements for the Governor's apartment were typical of what would face project staff over the next twenty years in developing period displays within the guidelines set in the original cabinet minutes, principally to provide to the public a

---

22   John Lunn, Interpretation - a Preliminary Report on the Fortress of
     Louisbourg National Historic Park, Ms. on file, Fortress of
     Louisbourg, Oct. 23, 1963, p. 9.

realistic representation of eighteenth-century material culture. The biggest and most immediate problem facing interpretation staff was the absence of furniture and furnishings appropriate to the 1740's period that was to be depicted in this particular and in other display environments. After the abandonment of the fortress and town in the 1760's the contents of buildings were either removed or destroyed and very little that survived into the middle of this century could be traced back directly to the colonial town.

By the mid-1960's the project was accustomed to engaging consultants for work that was beyond the capacity of staff in Louisbourg or elsewhere in Parks Canada.[24] For specialized curatorial services for interior work on the Governor's apartment and elsewhere in the reconstruction, Lunn engaged a consultant, Jean Palardy, a widely acknowledged antiquarian and expert on eighteenth-century furniture in Quebec and France and a close associate of Lunn's. This began a long association between Palardy and the Louisbourg project that was indispensable in building up the collections needed over the next twenty years of outdoor museum and historic site development.

Lunn and Palardy collaborated to complete the furnishing and interpretation of the Governor's Apartment in haste and with the assistance of project staff. The collections were acquired in France where Palardy worked as a collector and dealer for much of the year and in Quebec where he had worked for many years in association with other collectors and dealers as well as skilled artisans who could reproduce what could not be obtained on the antique market. For the governor's apartment he chose curatorial methods that would come to characterize the Louisbourg project for years to come, principly the combined use of original and reproduction furniture and furnishings, the eclectic and sometimes impulsive purchasing of large and small private collections and the minimal documentation accompanying many such acquisitions.

---

24 Fortress of Louisbourg Archives, Ms. by Sandra Fergusion, General Notes on Project Files, 1985, p. 10.

Palardy and another researcher, Yvette Theriault, studied primary documents concerning furniture and furnishings in the Kings Bastion and produced reports consisting mainly of notations on source material.[25] These sources, such as the DuQuesnel estate inventory, were used to compile acquisition lists for the purchase and reproduction of objects in 1965, although a comprehensive report on the construction and occupation of the King's Bastion was not completed until 1971.[26] In the interim Palardy relied on his own knowledge and experience and that of his associates to assemble a typological collection representative of the middle of the eighteenth century and earlier, for use in specific displays and for later use as period displays expanded. His work bridged the gap between research information and interpretation by accumulating collections while early planning efforts were underway. Two factors made this possible: the nature and extent of information available on the King's Bastion and the decision to focus the interpretation on the period just prior to the siege of 1745.

The Governor's wing of the King's Bastion was one of the most prominent and well documented buildings in the colony. In addition to the Governor's official residence it contained the garrison chapel, which served as the parish church, the meeting chambers for the governing council and accommodation for junior officers. Numerous official functions took place there. As the focal point for military, religious, legal and social activity the wing provided an excellent opportunity for the interpretation of a major cross-section of colonial

---

25 Palardy, Jean. Research in France concerning the furnishings of Chateau St. Louis, Louisbourg, Ms. on file, Fortress of Louisbourg Archives, file # AJ-24 and 25, Sept. 1964; Theriault, Yvette. Occupation - Destination - Ameublement du Chateau St. Louis, Louisbourg, Ms. on file, Fortress of Louisbourg Archives, 1965.

26 Adams, Blaine. "The Construction and Occupation of the Kings Bastion Barracks", Ms. on file, Fortress of Louisbourg Archives, July 1971; published in *Occasional Papers in Archaeology and History, contribution from the Fortress of Louisbourg #3.*

life, juxtaposed to the simplicity and squalor of the soldiers' barracks in the north wing of the same building. There was no question that the Governor's wing would be furnished to period, even if there was no estate inventory, and that decision did not require a formal planning process. The choice of 1744-45 as the period for furnishing and interpretation was equally obvious since the building exterior was reconstructed to that period. Without a formal planning process the project was nevertheless able to establish workable basic parameters on the foundation of earlier research and development decisions, which allowed interpretation work on the King's bastion to proceed.

While Jean Palardy acquired collections, John Lunn and his staff in interpretation and construction prepared the building for displays. The interpretation methods chosen made good use of current information technology without seriously compromising the period appearance of the building interior, thereby setting an important precedent for future displays. The use of audio tapes played on telephone head sets obviated the need for written texts and graphic panels which would have been more intrusive. The optional audio tapes carried an interesting selection of the wealth of historical information available without confusing or delaying visitors against their will; again without major visual distraction from the collections on display. Traffic barriers were constructed of solid pine with period finish and clear plexiglass inserts. This combination of historic and modern materials controlled visitor traffic without overwhelming or seriously distracting from the period decor, and allowed inclusion of display objects that otherwise would be unacceptably subject to damage or theft. The optional audio tapes carried an interesting selection of the wealth of historical information available without confusing or delaying visitors against their will; again without major visual distraction from the collections on display.

The decision to focus on the year prior to the 1745 siege imposed a major and convenient constraint on project planning and development, but one that imposed a character on the reconstruction that does not seem to have been fully debated. The context for

Louis XV furniture styles at Louisbourg would have been less questionable for a mere decade later because French residents then returning to Louisbourg after at least a four year hiatus in France would be much more likely to bring new furniture and furnishings with them. The early decision in favour of a pre-1745 representation of the historic site gave focus to the physical reconstruction and tied it to a truly significant though artificially precise era, but denied to the public visual evidence of the equally significant eras of the New England occupation and the second French occupation of the 1750s. Although some of the interpretation programmes have attempted to blend all of the decades of Louisbourg's colonial history in an evolutionary presentation, the actual reconstruction and to a large extent the costumed animation activities — the programmes with the highest development priority, tourism profile and visitor appeal — have been locked into an incredibly narrow slice of history.

The project correspondence and planning documents routinely refer to this major decision as a given that seems rarely to have been questioned, yet this is the very sort of selection process that is critical to all museum and historic site work. There is evidence that serious consideration was given to a more scattered reconstruction, one that would have 'selected' for research and development a series of substantial and impressive structures, mostly those of the military and civilian elite.

Task Force Planning

The decision to focus on 1744 and 1745 streamlined the planning process. The project, nevertheless, faced the furnishing and interpretation of dozens of complex display environments, as well as a costumed animation programme, expanded visitor information and security requirements and incorporation of modern services in a reconstruction area comprising more than 50 properties and nearly two miles of fortification features. Some of the basic decisions and policies were set into place and a major programme review resulted in Cabinet approval in 1969 for increased capital funding for the reconstruction, while annual operating budgets kept pace with completion of development in such locations as the Kings Bastion.

It was agreed that development should not proceed further, however, without a systematic plan and a special Parks Canada task force was appointed to complete and formally report on that process. John Lunn was appointed to the task force and he and the senior Louisbourg staff wrote and edited the task force documents approved in 1973. These reports, particularly the Interpretive Prospectus of April, 1972, have guided park development and operation since 1973.[27]

By March 31,1973 (the end of the Parks Canada financial year) approximately $16 million in capital funds had been spent on park development over 12 years and by October, 1974 the estimated total cost of completion was set at $23 million. The annual operating budget for the park increased to more than two million dollars by 1975, as new programmes came into operation.[28] The Task Force was asked to make recommendations for the completion of development and to provide the basis for long-range planning. Their deliberations were part of an overall effort to rationalize and consolidate the system of natural and historic parks and sites after a decade of unprecedented growth. They also coincided with the decentralization of many Parks Canada functions and services from Ottawa headquarters to five regional offices in Halifax, Quebec City, Cornwall (Ontario), Winnipeg, and Calgary. The Halifax office began to play a greater role in the development and operation of the Louisbourg project after this decentralization in 1975, but Louisbourg retained its own staff in most functional areas, including research.

---

27 Task Force Report, 1973 and Interpretive Prospectus, 1972, Mss. on file, Fortress of Louisbourg Archives.

28 Fortress of Louisbourg Archives, Ms. by Sandra Ferguson, General Notes on Project Files, 1985, p. 15-16.

The planning function and its professional staff were located in Halifax but it was established too late to play a significant role in the Louisbourg planning process. The job was left to Park Superintendent John Lunn and staff; the Director, Atlantic Regional Office, National and Historic Parks Branch, Halifax; Head of Interpretation and the Assistant Director (Historic Parks and Sites), Ottawa; with overall direction and approval provided by the Director, National and Historic Parks Branch, Ottawa.

The two most important reports prepared by the Task Force were the *Interpretive Prospectus* of April, 1972 and the *Recommended and Reduced Postures, Development and Operation and Maintenance*, April, 1973. Together they provided the blueprint for future research and development at Louisbourg. As planning documents the Prospectus was largely intended to be conceptual in scope, while the Recommended Postures provided the rudiments of a management plan for the park.

The extent of research undertaken during the first decade of the project was evident in the Interpretive Prospectus, written by John Lunn, which was replete with historical information.[29] Current politics, government influence and nationalist sentiments dominated in the prologue, which set a rhetorical tone that prevailed throughout the report:

> There will be some, no doubt, who think of Louisbourg only in terms of the glories of monarchical France or the triumph of British arms. But for most Canadians, Louisbourg stands as a proud symbol, not only of the two

---

29 John Lunn et al, " Interpretive Prospectus, Fortress of Louisbourg National Historic Park ", Ms. on file, Fortress of Louisbourg Archives, report # I-15, passim. The prospectus was the culmination of a series of interpretive planning reports written and submitted by John Lunn since 1970, which were ultimately synthesized and approved in the 1973 Task Force Interpretive Plan. All reports and related correspondence are available in the project archives.

great cultures whose interplay made our nation possible, but of the traditions that both have bequeathed to us. Without these disparate traditions and the dialogue stimulated by them, Canada would have few claims to nationhood.

These effusive references to Louisbourg's historical significance and to the philosophy that set the project underway in 1961 were seen as necessary to justify the extensive work completed or contemplated at Louisbourg. As the Parks Canada system expanded and heritage preservation achieved a higher profile across the country, the demand for heritage related activity increased, and within Parks Canada Louisbourg became both an inspiration and a conspicuous drain on resources. Competition for funding increased to the point where a veteran member of the Historic Sites and Monuments Board of Canada, Dr. P. B. Waite of Dalhousie University in Halifax, was reported to have remarked wryly that Nova Scotia was in danger of sinking into the Atlantic ocean under the weight of historic parks, sites and commemorative plaques.[30] As one of the oldest provinces, Nova Scotia had a legitimate claim to a seemingly disproportionate level of heritage development, but the rest of the country was just as anxious to catch up with their history after centennial year celebrations, and Louisbourg showed them what was possible. Within Nova Scotia other significant heritage resources such as the Halifax Defence Complex continued to deteriorate while the Louisbourg project prospered. The social and economic imperatives for the Louisbourg reconstruction prevailed, but the cultural and heritage arguments were beginning to wear thin by comparison to other areas. Consequently little effort was spared in the Interpretive Prospectus to justify continued development and to maximize its interpretive potential.

---

30 Reports of Professor Waite's remark circulated widely in the Research Section, Atlantic Regional Office, Halifax in May, 1975, at which time the author of this study was a member of the historical research staff.

Concerned about possible funding reductions, the prospectus emphasized in all too familiar terms the need "to provide the visitor with a convincing period experience." Reduction in the number of buildings to be reconstructed had been part of the approved strategy to concentrate on the buildings and fortifications of the King's Bastion, the Dauphin Demi-Bastion, the Piece-de-la-Grave and the town blocks within those features, "a sufficient area of reconstruction to enable the visitor to feel he has stepped back into a reasonably convincing facsimile of the past — but an area only *just* sufficient for that purpose — no more. This, in essence, is what is presented herein."[31] The project brief, rationalized and codified in the prospectus after a decade of development, included a modern visitor reception centre, service roads, and interpretation of historic and natural features outside the reconstruction area; these were clearly secondary to "re-creating a segment of 18th century life in colonial Louisbourg."[32]

Comparison of the Louisbourg planning process with another major project within Parks Canada, the Halifax Defence Complex, reveals that planning at Louisbourg from 1960 to 1975 was less sophisticated and less restrictive than planning at Halifax from 1975 to 1980, reflecting maturity on the part of Parks Canada, a growing public interest in its activities and a determination to learn from the best results achieved at Louisbourg.

The Management Plan for the Halifax Citadel National Historic Park was completed in 1979 and covered virtually every major aspect of site development, operation and maintenance in a document comprising 235 pages of text with accompanying plans and appendices.[33] Little was left to conjecture or dispute as the restoration proceeded and research staff were usually given sufficient time to

---

31 Lunn, op. cit., p. 2.

32 Ibid., p. 6 and appendices.

33 Halifax Defence Complex, Management Plan, Halifax Citadel, 1979.

complete reports prior to construction activity. The scope and the pace of research and development at the Halifax project was less than that for Louisbourg and less has been achieved, but the integration of research with other related activities has been consistent and well scheduled, partly as a result of the good and bad experience gained at Louisbourg.

CHAPTER 3
Programming & Interdisciplinary Work after 1973

Planning and development since 1961 had left a substantial legacy at Louisbourg after task force deliberations and reporting were completed in 1973. Reconstruction of fortifications and buildings in the Kings Bastion were complete and open to the public, the Dauphin Demi-Bastion and Quayside structures were already substantially complete, twenty two other buildings had been reconstructed, ten were in the process of design and reconstruction and work on fences, outbuildings and yards was either underway or planned. During the six month visitor season between May and October, 1973, 138 thousand people visited the remote historic site, even though its reconstruction was far from complete and no serious effort had been made to advertise or promote it as a tourist attraction.[1] Work progressed on the design and construction of an extensive new visitor reception centre, which was to be linked to the reconstruction area by an improved bus transit system (busses were

1   John Fortier, "Patterns of Research at Louisbourg: The Reconstruction Enters Its Second Decade", *Canada: An Historical Magazine,* Vol. 1, No. 4 (June 1974), p. 9.

already operating between a temporary reception centre and the Kings Bastion parade square). The visions of earlier planners and supporters of the Louisbourg project were finally beginning to take shape.

Consolidation of the planning process and confirmation of Louisbourg's place in the Parks Canada system had been overdue and was welcomed by those involved, but the challenge remained to develop new programmes and to improve existing operations within these newly approved frameworks. Consequently, programming at Louisbourg after 1973 proved to be just as busy and demanding as the planning and development phase had been since 1961.

Louisbourg's primary objective had been clearly enunciated in the Interpretive Prospectus, "to provide the visitor with a convincing period experience." The Louisbourg Task Force subsequently presented two options for pursuing this first objective, a recommended level of operation that would continue the current rate of development and operation for at least five years and a reduced level of operation that would, in essence, halt further development and limit operations programming to those properties that were substantially complete. The reduced level of operation was not presented as a realistic alternative. The task force report provided a list of the consequences that would be inherent in such a major curtailment of development and stated emphatically, once again with reference to the original political will of the federal government, that the project's potential for interpretation and education and its continuing role in the tourist economy of Cape Breton justified the high level of expenditures incurred since 1961, and warranted even more expenditures in the future. The following quotation from the task force report describes the consequences and because it provided a timely re-affirmation of the basic rationale for the Louisbourg project as expressed by the Cabinet in Ottawa in 1969:

"that the project will achieve the greatest possible historical impact and also produce the maximum tourist benefits."

"(that it) will rank as one of the most impressive and authentic historical reconstructions ever undertaken and will be an attraction comparable in almost every respect . . . with Williamsburg."

"(that it) will be one of the major tourist attractions in Canada and as such will result in an addition of a minimum of $10 million dollars annually to the economy of Cape Breton."

"The only way to achieve these goals is through the concept expressed as Program "B". Program "A" falls far short of fulfilling that concept in every significant regard, aesthetic, historical, and economic."[2]

The "concept" expressed in the recommended posture was ambitious, which the task force acknowledged in a somewhat subjective tone: "The showing will in fact be superior, for such is the nature of the Project."[3] The report also included, under the heading of long range planning and in a category described as "desirable but not essential", a list of additional historical properties and services that could be developed at a 1973 cost of almost three million dollars, an estimate that did not include expenditures for operation and maintenance.[4] The project had already reached proportions that demanded substantial expenditures to remain viable, let alone superior,

---

2   Louisbourg Task Force, Recommended and Reduced Postures, Development and O.&M.: (Plus Long Range Development Costs), April 12, 1973, Ms. on file, Fortress of Louisbourg Archives, unpaginated.

3   Louisbourg Task Force, Recommended and Reduced Postures, Development and O.&M.: (Plus Long Range Development Costs), April 12, 1973, Ms. on file, Fortress of Louisbourg Archives, unpaginated.

4   Ibid., concluding page.

and the task force submissions were obviously intended to justify and sustain the momentum generated since 1961.

The breakdown of forecast expenditures included in the task force report reflected the major changes that were occurring in project development and operation. As construction costs decreased expenditures for interpretation, visitor services and resource conservation increased.[5] These changes were also reflected in the recruitment, specialized training and in the management of project personnel during the transition from the planning and development phase to a fully operational park. Since the consolidation of all programmes under the direction of the Park Superintendent in 1965, the Louisbourg organization evolved as two separate programmes in terms of budgets and personnel. In theory the capital programme covered strictly developmental activity while the operation and maintenance programme included ongoing activities resulting from development. In practice, budgets and personnel were shared in a flexible organization based on teamwork principles.

In a speech delivered at the 1976 conference of the Canadian Museums Association, Park Superintendent John Lunn talked about teamwork:

> "I have lost most of my respect for those curators who are so obsessed by the mystique of their particular disciplines, that they fail to communicate with their institution's educators, interpreters or communicators until after their exhibits are installed. And I will never personally condone the hiring of a curator . . . unless I am certain that the curator knows what it means to work

---

5   The term visitor services was used interchangeably to describe capital programmes such as reconstruction of properties as well as direct services to visitors, for example guided tours, so expenditures in this area appeared in both capital and operation and maintenance forecasts.

as a member of an interdisciplinary team in the process of communication with a museum visitor."[6]

In a separate article the Head of Research at Louisbourg, John Fortier, expressed similar sentiments concerning researchers and their role in the research and development process:

"Every day they have to work with colleagues in different disciplines — architecture, archaeology, engineering, graphics, museology and administration — to solve specific design problems for projects that may cost two or three hundred thousand dollars to construct . . . General assertions and quick conclusions may be easy in a seminar . . . but it is surprising how that sense of confidence can disappear when there is a personal responsibility for guaranteeing that the details of a new building or exhibit are accurate before it is built."[7]

For both Lunn and Fortier, experience at Louisbourg had demonstrated the need and desirability of teamwork. The job was simply too complex to be pursued by individual units within the park organization, and the working environment at Louisbourg after relocation of the research staff was not conducive to individual or isolated effort.

In many respects the geographical isolation of the Louisbourg project from the mainstream of Parks Canada activities and programmes and from the academic and museum community in general — a condition that was not without historical precedent — was an advantage; especially during the long winter months from October to May when the park was closed to the public. This was particularly true as the Louisbourg organization became even more

---

6   John Lunn, "New Structures, New People, New Roles", *CMA Gazette,* 1977, p. 37-8.

7   Fortier, op. cit., p. 12.

self-sufficient and mature in terms of research and curatorial collections and in its ability to recruit, train and retain personnel. These circumstances allowed project management to concentrate organizational effort on those programmes that were approved within Parks Canada and at least known if not accepted by the local community.

Despite the scope of the project and the size of the staff, people knew each other on a personal basis and they also knew that they were working on a very important project. Those who did not grasp its historical significance could not escape its social and economic impact on a small local community of about 1400 people. The working environment and the community setting were suited to focus and teamwork, and park management encouraged this approach. On a formal and informal basis, park managers and professionals, as well as technical personnel and support staff shared and applied historical information and resources in a collective attempt to meet the objectives approved after the formal planning process was finally completed. The organizational structures and methods employed, especially the system of interdisciplinary committees and teams, provided the flexibility needed to progress from conceptual planning to implementation and programming.

This method of blending formal and informal networks in an intentionally designed interdisciplinary setting was not a common characteristic of large, traditional organizations, such as government agencies, in Canada or elsewhere during this period.[8] The prevailing government style of organization was not well suited to museums and historic sites, although many federal and provincial government sponsored institutions and agencies complied with this basic bureaucratic model. The development and use of blended and flexible organization at Louisbourg attracted attention within Parks Canada,

---

8   There is a wealth of literature that could support this statement on
     conventional organizational behavior during the period of this study.
     A good general reerence is: Allen R. Cohen, et al (eds.), *Effective
     Behavior n Organzations: Learning from the Interplay of Cases, Concepts
     and Student Experiences*, Homewood, Ill., R.D. Irwin. 1980.

was applied to the development of other historic sites in the system and served as a new model for local, provincial and national historic sites and outdoor museum villages in general.

Park Organization

The formal network consisted of a park organization that was typical of government agencies, hierarchical at the senior management level, strictly linear in its reporting relationships at the supervisory level, and task oriented at the technical and labouring level. Section Heads in Research, Administration, Engineering and Works, Interpretation, and Operations reported to the Park Superintendent, who reported to the Regional Director of Parks Canada in Halifax.

Unlike most museums in Canada, the park had no board of directors as such to determine policy and oversee park programmes. The Superintendent was accountable to Parks Canada executives in the Atlantic Regional Office, and through them to the senior executive levels of Parks Canada in Ottawa. All Superintendents met at an annual conference that concerned, among other matters, policy and programming at the national level. The conference was one of the best ways for Superintendents to remain abreast of major changes in policy and to ensure that appropriate changes were made in park programmes at the local level, so while they were not formally or directly involved in policy formulation beyond their own parks they were able to influence that policy through such mechanisms as the annual conference. This was particularly true for the Superintendents of the larger parks and sites like Louisbourg.

As one of the largest parks in the system by the early 1970s, Louisbourg was able to establish and carry out its own programming within the parameters set by the Task Force and under the authorization of Parks Canada executives. This arrangement left a large measure of control to the Park Superintendent and equally large scope for creativity and initiative by Louisbourg project staff.

Many of the achievements in programming after 1973 can be attributed to the park's capacity to function without a board of directors, without the necessity of raising funds outside the Parks Canada system and with the maturity to maintain its status as a national monument and tourist attraction. The system of committees and teams established to organize interdisciplinary work within the Louisbourg project and to provide a forum for new ideas had helped to get some of these new programmes established.

Committee and Team System

The four interdisciplinary committees established and functioning by 1975 were: Structural Design, Exhibits Design, Furnishings Design and Period Presentation. Each had a particular role to play in park development and operation, but there was some overlap as the following description of their activities will attempt to indicate. Some of that overlap resulted from difficulties in organizational terminology, such as the use of the term visitor services to cover reconstructed buildings and their services in the budget forecasts, but also to identify programmes such as living history and guided tours as a staff activity in personnel forecasts. Also, the terms interpretation and education were used broadly and properly to describe activities that cut across several organizational units and were the concern and responsibility of all staff. Much of the overlap occurred, however, because there were conflicting views within the Louisbourg project on how new programmes should develop. These conflicts were normal for such a large undertaking and they inevitably led to heated exchanges and wrangling during committee and team meetings, just as they did in other forums such as the section heads meetings. Without the committee system, however, some important ideas and issues would not have been discussed and debated to the extent that they were — such as in the early decision to focus the entire reconstruction on one year — and communication and progress could otherwise have been left to the inevitable vagaries and slow pace of the bureaucratic structure.

From the outset, meetings of these interdisciplinary committees and teams were well documented because a high priority was placed on research evidence as the basis for decisions. The minutes of their proceedings have been retained in the project archives. Apart from making fascinating reading, they provide an excellent source for charting the course of project development and they have served for the past 25 years or so as a continuing and required reference point for updating and verifying park programmes. Part of the rationale for the committee system was to provide a mechanism for future change in programmes as new research evidence and interpretations developed, but also to ensure that any change would take into account previous decisions and the basis for them, and that these changes would be further and similarly documented.

Structural Design

The Structural Design Committee was responsible for the design of all historic structures, not just buildings but outbuildings, yards, fences, streets, wells, wharves and, of course, all fortification features; as well as modern services and features that had to be concealed within the reconstructed properties. The terms of reference and the composition of the committee reveals that it was more important than the formal park organization as a vehicle for development at Louisbourg. The committee operated on two levels, the full committee level and the team level. The link to park management was established in full committee, chaired by the Park Superintendent and usually attended by all Section Heads. Their signing authority on all final drawings and specifications was required before reconstruction could proceed. In addition to ensuring this authority, full committee meetings provided a forum for discussion and debate of research findings, reconstruction methods and scheduling. Decisions were not always reached without time-consuming debate and occasional rancor, but the committee meetings, attended by representatives of all disciplines as equal voting members, produced results that could not have been achieved within the formal park organization.

Historians were normally assigned to conduct research on all of the buildings and properties on a town block and to report on that research within one year. In the case of Block 4, research on Lot A had to be conducted on an urgent basis in 1972 prior to the archaeological excavation of one of the buildings on the property, the Delort storehouse; a substantial and complicated structure scheduled for reconstruction beginning in 1973. In theory the historian would complete the research and ideally the report before the first archaeological field season. In practice the historian and archaeologist collaborated closely during the research phase and attended design meetings within weeks of commencing their research.[9] Excavation of the Delort Storehouse was underway before research for the entire block was assigned and structural design committee and team meetings began as soon as the archaeological field season was completed. Historical research for the remaining structures and properties on Block 4 was assigned in early 1973, by which time as-found field drawings of structures and features on Lot A were being prepared by reconstruction design staff in close collaboration with archaeological research staff, and these drawings were used immediately as the subject of design team meetings.

Invariably research staff left these meetings with a list of detailed questions to be investigated by consulting the evidence gathered up

---

9   Design team meetings for the Delort storehouse on Block 4 began eight days after this author's appointment to the project research staff in 1973, by which time I was already expected to contribute historical information and actively participate in its interpretation, after briefings by research colleagues and preliminary research conducted hastily in a surprisingly efficient archives organized for very specific purposes.

to that point. Days, sometimes weeks later, tentative conclusions would be brought to design team meetings, analyzed and if found to be valid, incorporated immediately into hasty sketches and preliminary designs. The system worked at its best when postulations based on historical evidence were confirmed or denied on the spot by archaeological evidence, when an archaeologist answered questions posed by an historian and vice versa and when the restoration architect attempted to bring all the evidence together — literally and visually on the spot — in the form of more sketches and measured drawings with the assistance of design staff.

The design of the Delort storehouse provides a good example to illustrate this point. The historical evidence, especially the maps and plans from the 1718-45 period established the exterior dimensions of the building, confirmed by archaeological excavation, and that the roof had two slopes, suggesting a one-and-one-half storey structure of uniform elevation along its entire length. The archaeological excavation, however, also revealed considerably more deposits of building materials, most particularly brick infill from the walls on the northern half of the storehouse. The final design approved by the structural design committee after considerable deliberation at the team level provided for a two-storey building at the north end of Lot A, joined together with a one storey structure near the south end of the property. Details such as door placements were determined almost entirely by archaeological evidence from the foundations of the storehouse, while windows at the north end and north-eastern corner of the building were based primarily on historical views drawn in 1731, on historical references to the use of the building and on the basis of the known commercial activities of its owner, Guillaume Delort, prior to 1745. This amalgam of direct historical and archaeological evidence, combined with knowledge of eighteenth-century architecture and construction techniques, allowed the structural design committee to guide an accurate design and reconstruction of yet another important building in the colonial town. This could only be accomplished by interdisciplinary work at the design team level.

Figure 5: 1975 aerial view of the reconstruction in progress, showing the completed King's Bastion. Source: FORTRESS OF LOUISBOURG. NATIONAL HISTORIC SITE (Parks Canada).

Not all structures on Block 4 were designed and reconstructed with such confidence and accuracy. A substantial building on Lot D proved to be much more difficult; and illustrative of the vexations encountered throughout the reconstruction process at Louisbourg. Between 1733 and 1735 a large L-shaped structure was built running north to south along the eastern boundary of the lot and east to west along the Rue du Quay near the waterfront. Only after close study of historical maps and plans and a variety of documentary sources could conclusions be drawn on the functions and usage of various sections of the building, which had to be reconstructed to appear as it stood prior to the 1745 siege. Very little definitive evidence was available on the structure, which was obscured by the Ile du Quay buildings on the historical views of the town. The extensive commercial and residential use of the building in the early 1740's and the equally extensive building materials excavated from the site indicated a substantial wood-frame structure of two storeys. Documentary and archaeological evidence also allowed precise location of chimneys, fireplaces and some walls and staircases, enough to infer the general layout of the interior and the placement of exterior windows and doors; then the educated guesswork started.

Historical plans clearly showed one ridge line along the middle of the roof while the documentary evidence referred to a mansard roof. Research had established that the English plans of the town and many of the French plans were not as comprehensive and detailed for Block 4 as they were for the fortifications and for the town blocks where public buildings stood, and that for any area of the fortress and town there were contradictions within the historical evidence that could not always be resolved by reference to archaeological evidence.

The progress facilitated by the structural design committee led to the creation of new committees as new programmes were established and existing programmes, mainly in interpretation, received more attention. While most of the project's energy was devoted to the reconstruction of buildings and to the completion and opening of the King's Bastion during the first decade, other programmes were either carried out in isolation or they were delayed until staff could be assigned to them. This was clearly reflected in research activity which was concentrated almost exclusively on buildings and properties until the reconstruction programme was sufficiently advanced to allow a shift in emphasis. In the early 1970's research staff started to work as closely with their colleagues in interpretation and visitor services as they had with their disciplinary counterparts in engineering and architecture since 1965. The committee and team system, therefore was extended to coordinate their efforts and to ensure that the results of new research were applied as rigorously as they had been in structural design.

Exhibits Design

Modern exhibits installed within reconstructed buildings were the responsibility of the exhibits design committee. This committee also developed displays at the modern visitor reception centre, in small exhibit pavilions at strategic locations where major historical structures were researched but not reconstructed, and near the ruins of historically significant individual properties outside the reconstructed area. This committee was not responsible for the building interiors that were furnished to period, or for the material requirements of outdoor features such as streets, gardens, wharves and military installations. Because the exhibits design committee and teams worked primarily with modern materials and techniques, research staff were less involved in the process, except when historical evidence was required or major intrusions on the historical environment were contemplated, in which case the Period Presentation Committee and park management were sure to be involved at the full committee level.

The usual approach to exhibit design was to identify a subject or theme, designate a space where it could be interpreted and then to conduct an investigation of pertinent historical information and artifacts that could be considered in the committee and team deliberations. Teams were chaired by the Curator of Exhibits, but most decisions were referred to full committee because the exhibits staff was small and isolated, because most of the exhibits had to take into account the accumulated knowledge and expertise that carried over from structural design and because park management took a particular interest in interpretation efforts that reached the visiting public directly. Also, the overlap of responsibilities among committees and staff units was best resolved at the full committee level where an attempt could be made to balance various period and modern interpretation methods.

All of these concerns made the work on exhibits design difficult and challenging and usually led to change and compromise at the committee level, often very late in the design process and sometimes during the installation phase. The problem was peculiar to Louisbourg where so much was invested in the reconstruction of a period environment and so much was expected in terms of visitor understanding and comfort. There was simply no opportunity for conventional exhibit design within the reconstructed area, so experimentation became necessary and normal, just as concealment of modern services had become in the structural design process. The following case studies underline the extent to which the Louisbourg project was developing unique interpretation methods in exhibits design.

An exhibit on eighteenth-century building construction and techniques at Louisbourg was installed in the Carrerot House on Block 2, a two-storey structure on a corner lot near the centre of the reconstruction area. Two major constraints led to innovation. To preserve the period exterior and the views from two streets, only period features and objects, mostly reconstructed or reproduced, were placed near windows and doors. Signage identifying the building and designating the exhibit was limited to a very small and inconspicuous label on the Rue Toulouse entrance door. All other labels and scripts were confined to the central interior of the Carrerot House where they could not be seen from the outside of the building.

A second constraint ensued from the exhibit theme, which called for exposure of construction techniques, in this case wood-framing, on the interior but not on the exterior of the structure. To achieve this important interpretation objective the interior framing and floor reconstruction was left open and exposed at the south-west corner of the structure as part of the exhibit. Visitors could see and appreciate these features and the surrounding interpretation in the middle of the exhibit, but not from the exterior vantage points on the Rue Royale. This was not conventional exhibit practice for museum or historic site interpretation.

An exhibit on another important theme, the Louisbourg garrison, was installed in the Duhaget House, near and in view of the King's Bastion, with its related military facilities such as the reconstructed barracks, officers' and governor's quarters and the garrison chapel. The same constraints encountered in the Carrerot House applied to the Duhaget location, in that the building was on a busy street within the reconstruction and the theme selected in this case called for information on the officers of the garrison, since Duhaget was a captain in the colonial marines. Again modern devices could not be viewed from the exterior and the exhibit employed similar methods to conceal them. But the challenge was to show in this particular location at least some glimpse of an officers life at home, without furnishing the house to period; an obvious interpretation objective to be met at several locations elsewhere in the reconstructed area. The combination of specialists on the Exhibits Design team ultimately designed and installed a blend of period and modern materials in a precise and deliberate fashion, in what was termed a neutral zone on the second floor of the building. This innovative approach respected the period character of the house and its military theme while conveying information to visitors via modern media in a comfortable setting.

Experience with the Duhaget House exhibit led interpretation staff to propose a series of theme lounges in period buildings to complement modern exhibits and to blend with strictly period environments. This was a major and welcome change in overall interpretation design at Louisbourg in the late 1970s, and one that clearly demonstrated the benefits of interdisciplinary work on exhibit design teams and committees. The effort was led by exhibits design staff with the encouragement of park management, but its acceptance by research and visitor services staff in full committee deliberations allowed all specialists to make their contributions on their own terms in the interest of accommodating twentieth-century materials and visitors to a reconstructed eighteenth-century environment. The happy results were a decrease in staff friction and a reduction in complaints from visitors about exhibit fatigue and general discomfort during prolonged tours of the reconstruction. Theme lounges also helped to support the work of Furnishings Design and Period Presentation committees and teams by conveying information and providing visitor amenities that could not be incorporated into period environments.[10]

Furnishings Design

The Furnishings Design Committee was responsible for reproduction furniture and furnishings required for exhibits and period environments. The park's collection of originals could not supply all requirements and the conditions for conservation and use of original historical objects in an outdoor museum setting necessitated a major effort to research, design and manufacture a wide range of reproductions as substitutes. Some had been commissioned in France and Quebec during earlier curatorial work on the King's Bastion interiors and were copied directly from originals in museum and private collections. Similarly many of the objects and documents reproduced under the auspices of the Furnishings Design Committee were based directly on originals in the park's research and curatorial collections. The majority of reproduction designs, however, have been based on an amalgam of archaeological, documentary and iconographic evidence from eighteenth-century source material, once again requiring interdisciplinary teamwork and approval procedures within the committee system. The results range in size and material composition from the largest calibers of reproduction cast-iron artillery to pewter and faience household wares, and in complexity from intricate costumes and fine furniture to simple wooden drumsticks.

One of the first designs approved by the Furnishings Design Committee was for reproduction artillery. The few original cannon that were available to the Louisbourg project were so damaged and corroded that they could not be mounted on the batteries of the reconstructed fortifications. Determining the quantity and location of the guns was not difficult because annual artillery lists were included in the official correspondence that survived from the eighteenth century, and a comprehensive report on Louisbourg artillery had been prepared by a project historian.[10] Decisions on the type and on design

---

10   T. LeGoff, "Artillery at Louisbourg", *Manuscript Report Series, No. 50*, Ottawa, Parks Canada, 1967.

detail, however, involved additional research, measured drawings of original guns and archaeological fragments, and close study of engraved plates from the Archives Nationale in Paris and from the Diderot encyclopedia.[11] Some of the same sources were used as the basis for the design of gun carriages and equipment such as rammers and sponges, all of which had to respect original material and workmanship while conforming to modern safety standards. The design drawings and specifications received close scrutiny from full committee because they were the first efforts to incorporate the same standards for research in furniture and furnishings design as had been followed for the research and design of buildings and properties.

Other reproductions went through a similar process of research and design, except when original objects or fragments were not available as a basis for design, which was often the case for the many wooden objects that had to be reproduced. For these designs extensive use was made of the Diderot encyclopedia and of the project's picture file of eighteenth-century visual art. Detailed specifications were worked out at the design team level in most instances, usually by illustrators and craftsmen and not by the researchers who had originally found the source material. Eventually a wider range of specialists became familiar with the iconographic source material available at Louisbourg, and the dialogue between designers and producers and the inherent learning curve approached the level that had been in place for structural design. The results were better reproductions and a more expeditious approval process.

As the collection of reproductions steadily increased and the need to work with producers outside the park required modification and in some cases outright rejection of objects reproduced, the need for a separate standards committee to monitor the production, use and sale of quality reproductions became apparent. With the creation of this committee the work of furnishings design teams and full committee could be limited to the completion and approval of

11   AN, G 5 series, and Diderot, op. cit.

drawings and specifications. Also, a separate material research and design unit was established in the research section to work on reproduction requirements. Their work on designs and with craftsmen inside and outside the park was validated by the Furnishings Design Committee, but required less scrutiny as the reproductions programme expanded and matured. Staff in this unit and members of furnishings design teams worked closely with the Standards Committee and with the Period Presentation Committee to coordinate the presentation and use of reproductions by visitor services staff.

The material requirements of visitor services staff in period environments increased dramatically in the late 1970s as additional historical properties within the reconstruction were opened to the public. The Louisbourg project would have had difficulty keeping pace with these demands even if the period displays were merely static as in most outdoor museums, with security and interpretation staff and volunteers dressed in modern clothing. With Louisbourg's commitment to "animating" the lessons of history by developing a full programme for the costumed animation of military and civilian life in the fortress and town, the supply problem became acute. For several years the extensive reproduction costume and accessories requirements for the military and civilian animation programme were beyond the project's capacity. The project simply could not provide authentic reproductions for all requirements. Despite this programming dilemma and in keeping with its sometimes conflicting mandates for preservation, interpretation and tourism, the project research and design staff with the help of other specialists in the Operations section persevered within period environments with a changing mix of competence, compromise, ingenuity and occasional guile. They provided for visitors a relatively convincing programme of living history each summer, while staffing inadequacies and furniture and furnishings depletions were either resolved or ignored by project management and staff.

Ultimately the presentation to the public suffered. As was the case with the reconstruction of buildings and properties in the late 1960's, gradual progress was made and the public began to see more than a construction site with a series of empty sets. And again in this renewed effort, the system of interdisciplinary committees and teams was the principal organizational mechanism for concentrating work on the project's new priorities in period presentation.

Period Presentation

The Period Presentation Committee was responsible for all historical collections and activities that was done and shown in period environments, the most important interpretation programme. Its scope of activities and displays to be researched, developed and operated was daunting.

A total of 9,356 types of objects were required for 63 different period environments at an estimated initial cost of one and one half million dollars.[12] Items used in the animation program such as reproduction costumes, weapons and tools would have to be replaced on a regular basis each year at additional cost, and new objects would have to be researched, designed and produced as period presentation teams and committees developed and approved new activities and displays. It was obvious that period presentation requirements would keep the Louisbourg project in a developmental phase for years beyond the operations review of 1978; the year in which the project was supposed to be substantially completed.

With reduced development came a substantial reduction in research staff and a corresponding increase in visitor services and maintenance staff. The project's commitment to research activity, however, did not change with this reorganization of working units, which was based in part on the conscious institutionalization of interdisciplinary work in the committee system, particularly in period presentation. Whereas research activity had been confined largely to

---

12 Fortress of Louisbourg Archives, Project file, Furnishings
    Requirements-Period Environments, 1978 operations review.

Figure 6: 1989 aerial view of the reconstruction of Dauphin Gate. This is the main entrance for visitors and one of the focal points for costumed animation of military activity. Source: FORTRESS OF LOUISBOURG, NATIONAL HISTORIC SITE (Parks Canada).

Figure 7: 1989 aerial view of the reconstruction of Frederic Gate and the waterfront. Source: FORTRESS OF LOUISBOURG, NATIONAL HISTORIC SITE (Parks Canada).

Figure 8: 1989 view of the reconstructed, entrance to the King's Bastion with servants and soldier in a costumed animation scene. Source: FORTRESS OF LOUISBOURG, NATIONAL HISTORIC SITE (Parks Canada).

the Research Section, through their representation on the Structural Design Committee and its teams, research for period presentation was shared by the new Historical Resources Section (combining staff in research, curatorial and exhibits services) and the expanded Operations Section with its increased number of qualified research and interpretation specialists. Even the committee chairmanship, appointed by the Park Superintendent, was open to senior staff in either section although it was usually held by the Head of Operations. One category of the committee's work, the preparation, approval and use of period presentation inventories, shows how the committee and its teams could cut across organizational lines of authority to meet goals that were common to both sections, and in the process could achieve objectives that were set for the entire project.

These period presentation inventories listed, described and verified, by reference to historical sources, all of the activities, events, historical personnages and objects appropriate to each period presentation environment. They provided the historical and modern contexts for static period displays and live animation, and in sum they provide a basis for the interpretation of the architecture, material culture and living conditions of the colonial fortress and town. It was an important assignment and one that had to be carried out expeditiously.

The main impetus for the preparation of the inventories came from the Head of Operations, William O'Shea, as Chairman of the Period Presentation Committee. He was an experienced member of staff, having served as Visitor Services Officer under Park Superintendent John Lunn. Though not a member of the project's research staff, O'Shea was well qualified academically as an anthropologist to lead this effort and, as the manager of the staff that had to deliver living history programmes directly to the public, he was acutely aware of the urgency that prevailed. As Chairman of Period Presentation he was able to enlist the support of research and curatorial staff outside the Operations Section and then directly apply the results. Once a format for the presentation of conclusions and evidence was established and approved, the work proceeded on a priority basis within the research section and on period presentation teams that involved all concerned specialists. Within several months the most needed inventories were ready for approval by full committee and, as with the reconstruction drawings and technical specifications previously approved by the Structural Design Committee and the Furnishings Design Committee, the results were in a format that could be put to use immediately by the people who had to implement the interpretation programme.

Louisbourg's flexible organization and more particularly its system of interdisciplinary teams and committees allowed working units to adjust workloads and share common goals. O'Shea later became the first Head of the new Historical Resources section, largely as a result of his leadership and participation in these interdisciplinary committees and teams and in the application of their work.

The preparation of period presentation inventories was just one example of how programming was carried out at Louisbourg after 1973, and the Period Presentation Committee was just one of several organizational mechanisms devised to make the transition from planning to development and from development to operation. The benefits of interdisciplinary work on the conceptual or intellectual level were transferred in this process to the level of practical application, and the efficacy of institutionalized teamwork was demonstrated on many occasions. The remainder of this study is concerned with the results of that process, comparisons of Louisbourg with other historic sites and outdoor museums, the position and influence of the project in historical preservation, interpretation and public history and the lessons to be learned from Louisbourg research and development.

CHAPTER 4

Reconstruction & Interpretation

Reconstruction of Historic Properties

The decisions on which properties would be reconstructed, as discussed in earlier chapters, were determined primarily on the basis of how much historical information was available and by the various interpretation objectives set for the project; principally the attempt to create a convincing precinct of the original fortress and town. Approximately one-third of the town fortifications and one-quarter of the town site properties within the original fortification trace have been reconstructed, comprising more than two miles of fortifications and 50 military and civilian buildings with associated features and yards. The resulting assemblage is decidedly European in its overall appearance, especially by comparison to other French and British colonial possessions in North America from the same period.

The cumulative effect is a striking contrast to the nineteenth and twentieth century properties that surround the reconstruction, and the usual impact on visitors and staff includes a curious sense of isolation from modern life. There is in those who actively decide to experience that break visually and psychologically, a discernible change in their sense of time and place and a heightened awareness of life in another era; much like the evocative visions and insights many visitors experience in old or ancient European cities and towns or in the ruins of ancient communities and cultures in the middle and far east. All of the senses and the intellect can be affected and despite the limitations of any attempt to bring the past to life, a very real and serious attempt can be made to 'experience' history.

It is the physical reconstruction of properties in a concentrated area that seeks to produce this living history effect, reinforced by period furnishing and costumed animation. The conventional and modern museum interpretation methods employed in the visitor centre and in other didactic exhibits and theme lounges throughout the reconstruction are not intended to produce or reinforce this special experience, and they sometimes detract from it. A visit to Louisbourg is intended to begin and end educationally and visually with a panoramic view of the entire reconstruction, and once within its depth and texture the visitor begins inevitably to draw contrasts with the modern age and to develop at least some insight into the segment of the past that Louisbourg represents. That segment, as pointed out in earlier chapters, is chronologically a very thin slice of history, but it has within that limitation a remarkable breadth, complexity and realism. Simply put, the Louisbourg reconstruction is a superb monument to the eighteenth century.

The accompanying aerial views of the reconstruction give some indication of the interpretation and education possibilities inherent in a reconstruction of such scale, proportion and density. Its eventual completion and its evolving presentation to the public formed the essence of Parks Canada's response to the initial brief from the Federal Government Cabinet in Ottawa, a response brought to realization in the early 1980's after two decades of extensive research and development on approved properties. The process of property development culminated in their exterior and interior completion, the concurrent operation of many properties and the planned and systematic preservation of the entire site. The reconstruction has combined with the various interpretation programmes to give three dimensional expression and visual impact to the labours of historical and archaeological research.

Within period environments such imperatives as visitor safety and traffic flow sometimes necessitated structural changes that were not authentic to the period and did not follow specifications that were documented by historical and archaeological research. For example, the dining room in the reconstructed Chief Engineer's Residence, which originally had only one doorway, includes a second doorway to accommodate modern visitor access and traffic flow, and the floors for the second storey of a number of period environments had to be strengthened to safely hold numbers of visitors far greater than those who would have occupied the original space.

Such compromises within reconstructed buildings were kept to a minimum, constructed in period style and appearance and are largely inconspicuous to visitors. Similarly, the modern services such as electrical and heating systems and fire prevention equipment were concealed, often ingeniously, behind period features and facades. As much as has been possible, what the visitor sees in period environments inside and outside the reconstructed buildings is an accurate representation of what is thought by research and interpretation staff to be the original appearance. The result is a comparatively realistic cross-section of eighteenth century architecture and material culture in an outdoor museum setting, one that is best appreciated and evaluated by studying the general art and architecture of the period as well as the local research conducted by project staff. The vast majority of visitors do not even attempt that comparative analysis or scrutiny, however, so they often develop misconceptions of history because they do not question or criticize the reconstruction, thereby failing to see it as just this generation's attempt to recreate the appearance of Louisbourg's past. They are usually so impressed by the depth and magnitude of the historic properties that they believe all of the reconstruction to be absolutely accurate and authentic history, and this has often been encouraged by effusive and sometimes poorly trained staff. The many small compromises with history become easily overlooked in period presentation environments just because everything looks old and historical and because obvious modern accretions have been avoided or obscured.

Some buildings were reconstructed to the exterior only, not to be opened to the public on a regular basis, which allowed such modern requirements as large transformers, fire trucks and modern building materials and supplies to be concealed within. On Town Blocks three and four and on the Ile du Quay at the eastern end of the waterfront, buildings that were not designated to contain modern services were reconstructed and finished to the exterior only, the interior left vacant and closed to the public. This compromise was made as the result of major funding cuts after 1978, which had the salient benefit of allowing project staff to concentrate and to consolidate efforts to furnish and otherwise interpret properties west of blocks three and four, without detracting from the overall impact of exterior reconstruction and cultural landscape interpretation.

On the exterior of buildings within the reconstruction area, underground water and electrical systems ensured that streets, yards and open spaces retained their period elevations and appearance, always after archaeological excavation was completed. Every attempt has been made to clear away traces of nineteenth and twentieth century occupation within and immediately surrounding the original fortress and town. This was also the rationale for the location and inconspicuous construction of the administration, staff, storehouse and workshops complex, as well as the visitor reception centre and staff accommodation which were miles away from the reconstruction area, once again to preserve and not to intrude upon the period appearance and atmosphere presented to the visiting public. As a result of these painstaking and at times extraordinarily costly efforts a convincing period setting was created which has served as the basis and the starting point for the park's interpretation and public history programmes.

Thematically, however, the reconstruction has been incomplete in its overall impact because of the superficial inclusion of shoreline fishing properties and associated buildings, features and technology. The textual and visual information on this important international commodity and on the ubiquitous presence of fishermen and cod in and around the local area was available in exhibits and literature and indicated in several reconstructed properties, but this is not enough to convey a balanced presentation of the theme. As discussed in chapter three, the period presentation of reconstructed properties and costumed animation is the principal interpretation medium. The fisheries theme has been largely relegated to secondary and supporting media, in contrast to the fortress theme which is reflected with such obvious impact in the miles of reconstructed fortifications. This historical omission in interpretation is exacerbated by the lack of project research on naval history at Louisbourg, which hampers even the secondary interpretation of the international cod fishery and marine life at the coastal community and colonial port. In such an extensive historical reconstruction this constitutes a major aberration in thematic interpretation which has only recently been addressed.

An American Museologist and Professor of Museum Studies wrote in 1980: " . . . what open-air museums are all about is theater . . .. Living history provides actors for the sets and, in its developed phases, drama as well."[1] The 'set' at Louisbourg is the physical reconstruction of historic properties in sufficient accuracy and proportion to support a full range of interpretation programmes for all but one major historical theme. Collections and properly trained and motivated members of interpretation staff are all that is needed to bring the Louisbourg of the eighteenth century to life and in the process to provide a measure of realism for interested visitors.

Historical Collections

Any set needs props. The historical collections accumulated at Louisbourg in the 1960's and 1970's covered the entire spectrum of eighteenth century material culture and social strata; from paintings

---

1   G. Ellis Burcaw, "Can history be too lively", *Museum Journal*, Vol. 80, No. 1 (June, 1980), p.5.

and tapestries to muskets and cannon, from coarse earthenware and pewter to ceramics and precious metals and in costume from simple fishermen's woolens to the silk and laces of the upper classes. An attempt was made by curatorial staff to follow the material culture and interpretation guidelines set by historical and archaeological research, but the realities of the collectors' market in Europe and North America, combined with reduced curatorial budgets in the later years of the project, circumscribed and constrained efforts to assemble a more comprehensive typological collection that could cover all historical contexts. Gaps had to be filled by purchasing and manufacturing reproductions based on originals, on archaeological artifacts and on the specifications provided by material research and design.

The result is a vast collection of largely ordinary, typical and at the time of the research and development phase, readily available military and domestic objects from the mid eighteenth century and earlier, both originals and reproductions, suitable for display in an outdoor museum environment. Very few original acquisitions were either rare or costly on the antique and collectors market, but the total collection of commonplace objects was purchased or reproduced at enormous cost (exceeding two million dollars). Since the opening of the King's Bastion the expanded furniture and furnishings, arms and armaments and costume collections have been augmented and spread throughout the period environments and in the other interpretation programmes to complement and enhance the impact of the property reconstructions.

Interpretation Programmes

Throughout this study the importance of period presentation as the principal medium of interpretation has been emphasized. The reconstruction and curatorial efforts of the 1960's and early 1970's were intended to provide the basis for a glimpse of military and civilian life in the fortress and town during the 1740's, not just a living history spectacle but a serious, contextual and well-researched interpretation programme utilizing properties, objects, people, plants and animals — a cultural landscape — to fully present the history of colonial Louisbourg. In an article on history museums written in 1980, Thomas J. Schlereth, then Director of American Studies at the University of Notre Dame, concluded that:

> Most visitors to a history museum, unlike visitors to an open-stack library, have little idea of the vast amount of historical evidence stored and cared for in history museums . . . . They do not . . . see all the collections. But they should be able to see more than they do now and . . . they should have access to using that material culture evidence that is part of their past.[2]

Schlereth refers to this landscape as "an amazing historical document" and refers to the classic study, *The Making of the English Landscape* , by W.G. Hoskins who aptly describes land and its artifacts as "the richest historical record we possess.[3] Louisbourg, through its period presentation programme was very much a part of this attempt to convey a rich sense of history and a visualization of a past landscape to the general public, and not just to specialized living history enthusiasts and scholars. In this and in other interpretation programmes Louisbourg was part of a larger effort to preserve, present and in the process popularize Canadian and local history.

There is an important distinction between attempts to create a cultural landscape and the more limited and selective method of presenting a "period room", as practiced in traditional museums in the United States and Europe, particularly Scandinavia, since the late

---

2   Thomas J. Schlereth, The History Behind, Within, and Outside the History Museum", *Curator*, Vol. 23, No. 4, 1980, p. 264.

3   As quoted in Ibid., p. 266.

nineteenth century. Edward P. Alexander, Director of Interpretation at Colonial Williamsburg, in a 1964 article about period rooms, links their development to the decorative arts and argues that Colonial Williamsburg and other comprehensive presentations of historical environments were the exception.[4] At Louisbourg and at other historic sites and outdoor museums, period rooms could be placed simultaneously in both a larger and a more specific historical context, and could be better understood in relationship to their human and natural environment. What made Louisbourg special and different from most other major historic sites and outdoor museums was that this reconstructed environment was on the same location as the original and, unlike Colonial Williamsburg which was also on its original site, Louisbourg has not been subsequently surrounded by a modern city. This isolation from the modern world has given the Louisbourg interpretation programme an exceptional opportunity to present history in its original context with minimal distraction.

Military animation was based directly on primary and secondary historical accounts and portrayed a poorly equipped and inadequately trained colonial garrison, avoiding the usual pageantry and precision paraded in many historic sites elsewhere in North America, often inaccurately, to impress tourists. Soldiers at eighteenth century Louisbourg were as likely to be working on the construction of the fortifications or as labourers in the town as they were to be on guard duty, and they often got drunk. Also, their officers were as concerned with their commercial involvements and with selling liquor to their soldiers in officially sanctioned canteens as they were with military affairs and the regimentation of troops in their garrison.[5] The historical record also reveals that all ranks of the military

---

4   Edward P. Alexander, "Artistic and Historical Period Rooms", . *Curator*, Vol. V11, No.4 (1964), pp. 263-81.

5   Robert J. Morgan and Terrence D. MacLean, " Social Structure and Life at Louisbourg ", *Canada, An Historical Magazine*, Vol.1, No. 4 (June,1974), pp. 60-75.

were closely integrated with their equivalent classes in the civilian population. The soldiers' daily routine, therefore, has been depicted in association with servants and domestics in the town's reconstructed houses and public houses (inns and cabarets), and not confined to musket drills and cannon firing ceremonies. The result is a more realistic reflection and accurate representation of military life as it has been described in historical accounts.

Civilian animation is even more diverse and also attempts to represent everyday life, especially the lower classes at work, juxtaposed with soldiers and fisherman engaged in activities that were commonplace in eighteenth century Louisbourg and well described in court records and contemporary accounts. Cooking, serving and cleaning predominate and these activities allow the project to carry out routine housekeeping and security for historic properties as part of the interpretation programme. Special events such as the re-enactment of auctions in the street, regular and sometimes special and ceremonial meals in official and domestic settings, musical performances and games provide the opportunity to portray the upper classes in the costumed animation programme, and in the process to give visitors vignettes of life in all classes of colonial society.

The animation programme and period presentation environments in general focus on the early 1740s and draw on a wealth of information available in primary and secondary sources for the years preceding the first siege in 1745. As they did with structural design, historians participated directly in the period presentation teams and committees as the animation programme developed, ensuring again that interpretation was based on direct historical evidence wherever possible and informed appreciation of eighteenth century customs and manners.

Period food services were developed in the late-1970's as quasi-period presentation environments, where most but not all of the guidelines for authenticity applied, including the requirement for historical research input during the development phase. Concessions were made, however, in the incorporation of modern food services equipment in spaces concealed from the public, in eighteenth century recipes that had to be adapted to modern health regulations and the availability of food supplies, in serving arrangements that had to take museum visitors into account as patrons, and in the hiring and training of staff who would appear in period costume.

Four food service outlets were developed in historic properties that served similar functions in eighteenth- century Louisbourg: the Garrison Bakery, Hotel de La Marine, L'Auberge Seigneur and the Cafe Destouche. All four were contracted to outside agencies, initially the Cape Breton Development Corporation because of its involvement in tourism and eventually to the Fortress of Louisbourg Volunteers Association, essentially on lease arrangements under Parks Canada control.

The Volunteers association eventually became the preferred contractor because it was established as a non-profit society sharing objectives with the park, making it more sympathetic to park policy and hence more likely to pursue the same interpretation objectives. The beneficial result has been the provision of important services to visitors in environments that blend with period presentation, usually without seriously detracting from the principal interpretation themes and objectives set for the reconstruction.

Interpretation themes were not formally set until final preparations were underway for the opening of the modern visitor reception centre in 1976, though they had been implicit in planning documents throughout the 1960's and in the 1973 task force report. The well documented and at times complicated history of the fortress and town left many interpretation staff with too much information and without a manageable conceptual or thematic model to organize their thoughts and perceptions about Louisbourg's history. To avoid the factual errors and historiographical misconceptions that had been conveyed to the public, many of them gleaned in the park's own training programmes and scattered exhibits, a simpler six-theme model was established and approved to guide interpretation and training. In addition to serving as a conceptual model for staff and the visiting public the themes encouraged more effective extension programming and promotional activity

All six themes were to be interpreted in an introductory manner in the reception centre using small static displays with very few artifacts, supported by an extensive slide show in a four-section audio-visual theatre, and in more depth within the reconstruction using the various media, including audio-visual techniques in the modern exhibits and theme lounges. There was no attempt to allocate specific themes to any given media, except in a negative sense in the various period environments where modern techniques, especially audio-visual, were not to be considered and where the underlying assumption was that all themes would be represented in a more cumulative period presentation. The methods used in period environments, period displays and animation excluded all other methods in order to achieve the desired impact of the reconstruction.

The themes remained the same from 1976 until their consolidation in training manuals in 1981, but the changing sequence in which they were listed reflected changes in how research and development had evolved over the two decades, how interpretation staff variously perceived the history of Louisbourg and ultimately how the site was explained to the public as the interpretation and visitor services programmes evolved.[6] When first established, the military themes led the list, with prominence accorded to Louisbourg as a Fortress and Louisbourg as a Naval Port. By 1981 the sequence was as follows:

LOUISBOURG AS A CAPITAL
LOUISBOURG AS A FISHING BASE
LOUISBOURG AS A TRADING CENTRE
LOUISBOURG AS A FORTRESS
LOUISBOURG AS A NAVAL PORT
LOUISBOURG AS A COMMUNITY

---

6   A Louisbourg Primer: An Introductory Manual to the Fortress of Louisbourg National Historic Park, Ms. on file, Fortress of Louisbourg, passim.

Years of social history research by project historians were having the desired effect as a balanced view of Louisbourg's military, architectural, economic and social history emerged. Interpretation programmes were then developed on the basis of this important historiographical progress, which served to simplify and validate Louisbourg history as explained to visitors and to make it more accurate and interesting. Consequently, the authenticity of the reconstruction and historical collections was less compromised in its interpretation through secondary exhibits, theme lounges, publications and other educational programming.

As early as 1963 the need for comprehensive interpretation programming at Louisbourg was recognized: "Interpretation needs to be done here on a greater scale than anything previously attempted at any National Park or Historic Site in Canada."[7] What the Park Superintendent, John Lunn, meant by interpretation and what most Canadian museums practiced at this time was the traditional display, with cases containing natural specimens or historical collections which were explained by labels and scripts, often supplemented by models or audio-visual aids. Period rooms and at Louisbourg larger period environments were not yet paramount in the minds of designers and writers, and Louisbourg did not yet provide the resources to develop period presentation fully. Also, the required consolidation of interpretation themes for the Louisbourg project was not attempted until task force deliberations in 1972-73 clarified project objectives, which then required more focus in interpretation programmes. Consequently, stated themes and objectives, the critical first stage in interpretation planning and implementation, were not available to guide programming until the mid-1970's.

Scattered exhibits on sometimes disjointed subjects and themes characterized the interpretation programme in its first decade, while research, design and reconstruction of historic properties proceeded. These temporary exhibits were concentrated in temporary exhibit

---

7   Interpretation — Implementation ", John Lunn to A.D. Perry,
    9 December, 1963, p.2, Ms. on file at the Fortress of Louisbourg.

buildings, including an old schoolhouse that served as an interim visitor reception centre, outside the reconstruction area. Their design, preparation and installation rarely involved research staff. Most of these temporary exhibits were replaced after 1975 by permanent exhibits in the new visitor reception centre and in designated period buildings within the reconstruction. Except for several excellent scale models of fortification features and some occasional use of historical views and quotations, these were poor exhibits and they help to explain why the reconstruction process itself became so popular with visitors as the 1960s phase of the project progressed. This early interpretation work served an important museographical purpose, however, because it allowed the development and retention of technical staff who became more skilled with practice and more familiar with Louisbourg's natural and human history as a basis for later work with research staff on a renewed exhibits programme.

The Louisbourg project and Parks Canada in general had changed its exhibits philosophy by this time, as articulated in an approved Parks Canada Policy in 1979:

> The interpretation program for a national historic park will be based on the historical resources at the park and the themes of Canadian history which they illustrate . . . . Modern interpretation techniques may be used to give park visitors historical background, detail and perspective.[8]

Modern exhibits were clearly intended to support and not to overwhelm the presentation of historical resources in their original context, which confirmed and validated the approach taken at Louisbourg to emphasize and rely upon period presentation as the principal interpretation method. This debate on media selection was not confined to Louisbourg and Parks Canada. On museographical practice, specifically the use of audio-visual media, Josef Benes in a 1976 article published in an American museums journal wrote:

8 *Parks Canada Policy*, Parks Canada, Ottawa, 1979, p. 31.

"Museums will not, therefore, be turned into shrines of modern technology but will retain their own style of presentation in which audio-visual media will play only an auxiliary role, a role which will nevertheless increase the educational effectiveness of exhibits. This is a fundamental principle."[9] In another article written in 1979, M.B. Alt, then Head of Visitor Resources for the British Museum of Natural History, drew the debate into general museological focus with the following statement:

> The objects versus-story controversy has become something of a hoary chestnut in the museum world and the arguments are sterile. Those with more open minds put this polemic to one side and start from the premise that audio-visuals may enhance the museum experience; that is, they are legitimate and appropriate media for museums to use in certain circumstances.[10]

The consensus at Louisbourg was that those circumstances were very limited and at the least confined to areas outside the period environments. Where did that leave the exhibits programme? Already the research and exhibits design staff had to work within the difficult space and view planes limitations of reconstructed buildings and in accordance with period presentation guidelines. The new Parks Canada philosophy and its interpretation policy reinforced the requirement that all exhibits blend with period environments and support approved themes, yet still discharge the responsibility of conveying information to modern visitors using modern communication techniques. The research and curatorial collections available and selected for inclusion in exhibits helped in efforts to provide the

---

9   Josef Benes, "Audio-visual media in museums", *Museum*, Vol. XXVIII, No. 2, 1976, 121-122.

10   Josef Benes, "Audio-visual media in museums", *Museum*, Vol. XXVIII, No. 2, 1976, 121-122.

three-dimensional and graphic materials necessary in the design of background exhibits, and the team and committee system ensured that research staff were involved in this supportive interpretation role as they participated in decision making throughout the process. Archaeological artifacts and period prints, drawings and documents were usually included, always selected in accordance with exhibit storylines, and graphics consisted mainly of reproductions of eighteenth century iconographic source material. Even case designs utilized period motifs and were custom-built by staff preparators. Modern lighting, labels and scripts and the local production and use of audio tapes clearly distinguished these thematic exhibits, didactic displays and signage from period environments, but usually without overwhelming or seriously detracting from them. At the same time these exhibits were able to provide some of the general information necessary to place Louisbourg's history in the wider context of North American and European history. As well, they were useful for staff training because they brought together in convenient locations information that interpretation staff needed to know.

Exhibit environments also provided the opportunity to provide visitor comforts and amenities that could not be incorporated into period environments. As the reconstruction expanded in the late 1970's museum fatigue and information overload became serious problems. Theme lounges were developed in strategic locations where comfort and passive communication prevailed over active interpretation, and where sharp contrast between period and modern visual and psychological impacts was neutralized. Modern and reproduction furniture were mixed together and optional readings and relevant films were made available to those visitors who wished to inquire further on specific topics and themes. Where numbers have permitted, interpretation staff in modern dress have been made available to answer questions and encourage visitors to relax in comfort.

Interpretation staff in modern dress have also provided guided tours in special geographical areas and on specialized subjects, such as fortifications and architecture, again as an option to visitors who normally prefer to tour on their own and at their own pace. A self-guiding ruins walk through the historic area which was outside the main reconstruction area but within the original fortress and town, utilized ground level interpretation signage and has been popular with visitors since its completion in the early 1980's. It has been successful as an adjunct to the reconstruction because it is not so demanding on the senses and the mind and because it allows a clearer view of natural resources such as vegetation growth and coastal formation and erosion. The standard school tour packages for students and teachers and special tours for such groups as historical societies have always been a part of the park's interpretation programmes, and have, of course, included distribution of current interpretation literature.

Research and interpretation literature has been made available to the public in theme lounges and at a retail sales outlet operated for Parks Canada by the Volunteers Association in the visitor reception centre. Most of the titles fall into the category of popular history and a number of them were prepared by Louisbourg staff historians to support interpretation and staff training programmes. Illustrated interpretation brochures, information sheets and tour leaflets have been prepared almost on an annual basis and widely distributed to visitors to assist their visit, and a comprehensive and illustrated guide to historic properties was prepared in 1980 for sale to visitors. All literature is made available in both official languages, but is usually written in English and then translated into French, which has caused problems in communicating context and specialized terminology. These problems are minor because such literature plays a secondary role in interpretation at Louisbourg, serving merely to introduce the reconstruction and to convey practical suggestions to maximize the educational effectiveness and physical comfort of a visit.

The same literature has also been sent in advance to schools, tourist agencies and tour operators to prepare visitors for the opportunities and complexities of the Louisbourg reconstruction and its interpretation. As the project progressed from development to operation as a historic site and outdoor museum, more was expected of the park from the visiting public and particularly from tourism agencies, and from entrepreneurs who looked to Louisbourg as the major tourist attraction in the area and as a boost to the local economy.

The popularity of Louisbourg interpretation programmes improved at considerable financial cost throughout the research and development phase of the project and helped to determine how many people visited and how long they stayed, which were principal factors in the generation of revenue for the tourism sector. Visitation levels increased steadily and eventually leveled off in the early 1980s at about 150,000 annually in a four month season, despite Louisbourg's isolated geographical isolation and very little marketing and promotion. As one of the leading heritage attractions in North America, developed at considerable cost to the Canadian public, the Louisbourg reconstruction had to be operated and continuously maintained to the same high standards set during the research and development phase, including the commitment to research and interdisciplinarity that has characterized the project since 1961. The range of interpretation programmes based on that research and development process and its inherent balance of period and modern techniques has allowed the Louisbourg reconstruction to find its place among the leading historic sites and outdoor museums of the western world.

CHAPTER 5
Public History

American historian and museum commentator Jay Anderson, in a 1984 book on living history museums published after visits to Louisbourg, Williamsburg, and numerous other outdoor museums and historic sites throughout North America and in Europe, wrote:

> Living history is the only mode of historical interpretation, research, and celebration that involves all the senses. As such it forces us to experience the past as fully as possible. Of course, we can never be certain that the sights, sounds, tastes, textures, and smells of our re-created accounts of the past are authentic. The best we can do is to carry out our research as rigorously as possible and resist the temptation to claim too much for our time machines . . . Living history lies outside the boundary of established academic and public history . . . Each museum, each project, and each unit makes its own covenant with historical truth and determines the way it will carry on its dialogue with the past.[1]

---

1 Jay Anderson, *Time Machines: The World of Living History*, American Association for State and Local History, Nashville, 1984, p. 191.

In the same book Anderson had earlier praised Williamsburg and Louisbourg for having the most complete research data bases of any historic sites in North America.[2] This study supports his emphasis on the inextricable and strong link between research and interpretation. In many respects the Louisbourg project has been a case study and prototype of how to balance the two museum and historic site activities in the interest of both preservation and high public history standards.

Though such fundamental lessons can be learned from the development of large and well funded museum projects such as Louisbourg, it is also important to support conclusions in the fields of outdoor museums and historic sites development by studying different and particularly smaller institutions. Some general conclusions and additional object lessons concerning interpretation and public history are based on some of the practices prevalent at large and small museums and historic sites that have been visited and observed by the author.

Until recently there has not been a concerted effort by Parks Canada and what has become the English Heritage Agency to present history to the public in a proactive manner in museums and historic sites. The norm had been to display what constitute some of the best collections in the world with no more than supporting texts and publications, with exhibits that sometimes incorporated audio visual techniques. In North America in general, particularly in the United States, there has been an exceptional effort at places such as Williamsburg to present history to the public in a fuller context as an amalgam of European, aboriginal and African traditions, with guides and costumed staff providing an active interpretation of both the natural and cultural environment. Parks Canada's Halifax Citadel project and a variety of provincial historic sites have followed this example in their own interpretation programmes. These efforts have been emulated and extended in various ways in provincial and state capitals, in most urban communities and in many rural areas where

2   Ibid., p. 61.

significant historical resources are located. As discussed in previous chapters, Louisbourg has often been the point of comparison and justification for many of these new projects.

> The reconstruction's greatest legacy is, perhaps, the research, development and interpretive systems that were introduced and tested at Louisbourg, for these systems have subsequently been adopted as standard practice not only by the Parks Canada system, but by historic restorations in many parts of the world.[3]

The overwhelmingly positive public response to such projects and the economic benefits to the tourism economy are often the principal justifications for significant resource allocations, particularly by governments. The cumulative effect in the United States and to a lesser extent in England and Canada has been a more vigorous pursuit of public history. The more traditional and less active pursuit of history that still prevails at some British and Canadian museums and historic sites is yet another example of how different cultures present their history in different ways. This pattern of research and development produces different project objectives and standards of operation, in essence different agendas. Any comparison of these various approaches or attempts to draw museological lessons from them must first consider these different purposes, which in some cases involve fundamentally different philosophical and operational principles. The examples and case studies that follow are intended to amplify this assertion.

The reconstructed fortifications of Louisbourg bear some physical resemblance to the original, seventeenth century coastal defenses and fortifications that have been preserved at Berwick-Upon-Tweed, on the Northumberland coast of England near the Scottish border. Both extensive systems of fortification were based on the bastion

---

3   John Lunn interview by Terry MacLean, Louisbourg and Sydney, Nova Scotia, 19 August 1993.

trace and the use of smooth bore artillery, and both were designed to withstand a naval assault. In museological terms, the resemblance ends there. There had been at the time of my visits in the mid 1980s far less active interpretation at Berwick and very little promotion of it as a historic site. It is obvious that the priority has been placed on preservation, not interpretation.

There is, however, an important lesson to be learned from this particular case study. Institutions with limited funds to spend and historically significant resources to maintain sometimes need to confirm in their programming that one of the first and most important concepts in the generally accepted definitions of museums is preservation; the proverbial maxims of collection, preservation, study and presentation that guide good museum theory and practice were not necessarily meant to carry equal emphasis. Louisbourg's national significance historically and museologically — and the anticipated benefits to the tourism economy — may justify the many millions of dollars spent over the past three decades on both preservation and interpretation, but that large-scale approach to outdoor museum and historic site development has to be selective if the benefits of public history are to reach a larger spectrum of the regional, national and international public.

There are many small military sites in Canada, some within the Parks Canada system, that have been preserved and left in a relatively undeveloped state even when funds have been available and convincing economic arguments have been presented for comprehensive, tourism related programming. They remain largely mute in their witness to history, but like Berwick they nevertheless occupy an important place in the preservation movement and in the public history landscape.

The funds have not been available to apply the Louisbourg methods of interpretation to all of the historic sites and parks in the Parks Canada system and elsewhere. There are, however, other examples of outdoor museums and historic sites in Canada and in England where not enough money and time has been made available to develop interpretation programmes to an appropriate scale and with the effectiveness of Louisbourg and Williamsburg, usually because these smaller institutions work with different mandates and fewer resources.

The best museums and historic sites seek to ensure a balance between preservation and interpretation and to present the results in a manner that is comprehensible to the general public. There is always a measure of conjecture and creation, which is part of the historical interpretation process to which visitors will add their own subjective impressions. The end result in terms of public history experiences varies from group to group and from individual to individual in a process of informed intellectual and sensory inquiry. Interpretation becomes shared between the institution and the visitor, where the aim of the museum or historic site is not necessarily to instruct, but to provoke inquiry.

Outdoor museums have a special opportunity to interpret and educate in open, less congested environments. With proper planning and adequate staff support the collections and the visitors can be dispersed, allowing the contemplation of nature and the works of human cultures in an unfettered and non-coercive educational setting. This ideal balance between collections and the setting in which they are displayed and appreciated, and in the process explained in a broader historical context, is the essence of good outdoor museum interpretation.

Traditional gallery museums often have the same opportunity to interpret collections. The Musee de La Marine in Paris has a direct thematic connection to Louisbourg as one of the leading institutions in Europe that had provided source material for the research and development phase at the project, because it is one of the main repositories for the collections of the French Ministry of the Marine, the department which administered the colonies, including Isle Royale. The Musee can also be compared in museological terms to other maritime museums such as Greenwich, England. As at Greenwich, much is on display from world class art collections at the Musee de La Marine. The natural, architectural and material culture surroundings along the Seine in Paris, however, can have an additional and thematically relevant impact before the visitor enters the museum. The main collections of marine art and artifacts in the museum are relatively dispersed and can be studied on their own by theme, category and chronology. This is especially true of the Vernet port scenes of coastal cities in France in the eighteenth century which have been invaluable in comparative studies of the Louisbourg harbour and waterfront. Consequently there is a clearly articulated and broader context for the meanings conveyed by the marine collections on display, whereas the Greenwich museum, relatively isolated from the port city of London, has a more limited set of interpretation options.

The contrast of interpretation at these two major maritime museums raises the issue of how museums choose interpretation methods. A much smaller Maritime Museum of the Atlantic in Halifax, Canada, with collections and themes that derive largely from England and France as well as Nova Scotia, utilizes (in addition to its conventional exhibits) an interpretation method of simply displaying reserve collections to visitors, without labels, scripts or any other attempt to have the objects do other than speak for themselves. This is a valid insight into what the museum is trying to accomplish in collections research and education programmes. At the Halifax museum, however, informed staff are available to explain the collections and to answer questions, and all staff — including the director and curators — work a weekly shift on guided tours for the public.

The methods of preserving natural and cultural heritage vary from nation to nation and within nations, and the challenge to compete with such modern technologies and thematic derivatives as Disneyland and its fantasy clones, have their place alongside the original remains of our past, so evident in Europe and in so many other parts of the world. The essence of good museology, is to preserve the old and to develop interpretation programmes that utilize the new methods available. Preservation of extant remains and equal efforts to preserve their story — their documentation and interpretation — can teach the lessons of history in many ways, and to many people who would otherwise be excluded from this public history process of inquiry.

Oral tradition, is exceedingly important in the research of societies and communities throughout the world, and studies of linguistics and folklore have found their place museums where the story of ordinary people is documented and presented. These oral history interviews have been essential in their research, and audio selections from these interviews could be used effectively as part of the interpretation programme. Louisbourg does not have this interpretation option, but the statements of ordinary folk are recorded in the text of court proceedings, and these are extensively quoted in exhibits and animation scenarios. This is just one example of how the combination of research and curatorial methods can determine the range of interpretation options open to the museum or historic site.

The effort at Louisbourg to document and present the material culture of a colonial capital which developed originally without newspapers, photography or tape recorders and to represent a material culture on the basis of relatively scant original remains, except for archaeological artifacts, has posed special curatorial demands. Meeting those demands has required the use of a combination of documentary source material, period art and cartography and archaeological artifacts, with qualified interdisciplinary researchers working together to resolve the many contradictions inherent in the overall curatorial effort, and in the process to provide sufficient information to guide interpretation. The balance struck between Louisbourg research and interpretation programmes, has been made possible by an enormous investment of financial and human resources and by continuous efforts to keep all disciplines and work groups involved in a collaborative process.

Striking this balance is not an easy task for small museums, historic sites and nature reserves that usually lack the funds necessary to preserve and to fully interpret their collections, because many cannot generate sufficient revenue from admissions and retail sales to offset operating costs. After Louisbourg and other large parks and sites in the Canadian system became a major drain on the financial resources

129

of Parks Canada, new capital development projects proposed in the department's financial and personnel forecasts began to be assessed in terms of their *"operations and maintenance appetite"*. If funding could not be reliably estimated and justified for the long term operation and maintenance of the resource to an empirically established and acceptable standard, the capital project was unlikely to be approved. This policy particularly applied during periods of fiscal restraint. In this resource allocation and budgetary process, as systems planning and policy formulation advanced in sophistication and impact, Parks Canada's primary preservation requirements were to prevail over all associated interpretation and education programming, and this inherent assignment of priorities was formalized in a national policy document approved by the Parliament of Canada in1980.[4]

There is another important lesson to be learned by other small and large museums, historic sites and galleries from this Parks Canada experience in systematically setting priorities that balance preservation and interpretation. Too little attention to the quality standards of interpretation can also constitute a problem. An example of this pattern of development is provided at Bosworth field near Leicester, England, where the site of the Battle of Bosworth in August, 1485 is commemorated in a network of signage, footpaths and exhibits. Ground interpretation is supplemented by an excellent account of the battle and its historical significance.[5] During a visit to the site in 1982 it was difficult to conjure up a vision of events on the broad scale depicted in the historical account, studied closely prior to the visit. The exhibits were not self explanatory and the publication was not available at the visitor centre, a facility which was somewhat haphazardly accommodated in converted farm build-

---

4   *Parks Canada Policy*, published under the authority of the Minister of the Environment, Ottawa, 1980.

5   Williams, D. T., *The Battle of Bosworth*, Leicester, Leicester University Press, 1973.

ings. Ground level signage on the footpaths effectively interpreted battle tactics but ignored the wider historical context, and an audio-visual model of the battlefield, located in one room of the visitor centre and isolated from the main battlefield, was in need of repair and maintenance. As with many private and local authority museums in Britain, live interpretation by informed staff or volunteers was not provided.

An example of interpretation taking precedence over preservation has been provided at the Alexander Graham Bell Museum Complex in Baddeck, Nova Scotia, 75 miles from Louisbourg and also developed and administered by Parks Canada. At times in Parks Canada's development, particularly in the expansionist days of the late 1970s when public funds nationalist rhetoric matched a disproportionate amount of resources were allocated to nationally popular interpretation projects at the expense of preservation and collections management. The exhibits at Baddeck, which were approved and designed in Ottawa largely in isolation from local museum management and staff, provide a prime example. Hundreds of reproduction photographs and voluminous reams of interpretive scripts and graphics in the first two of three large galleries provide far too much information for the average visitor or for children to absorb. In total they confuse the history of Bell, his family and associates and their many achievements in science, technology and humanitarian endeavors. Many important artifacts and documents are either not on display or are obscured by modern interpretation methods. Within several years of their completion, serious deficiencies in the conservation of the Alexander Graham Bell family collections had to be recognized and their conservation adequately funded at the Baddeck museum. As a large, national organization with a serious commitment to conservation and with the professional and the technical resources to rectify this imbalance, Parks Canada was able to adjust its programmes at the Baddeck museum during the early 1980s. More attention was devoted to collections management, including the development of a systematic plan to rationalize and improve

their presentation to the public in a research and interpretation renewal effort that continues to this day.

Louisbourg and other large, mature and adequately funded institutions have made a significant and lasting contribution to the
development of museological standards for outdoor museums and
historic sites in Europe and North America. Collectively they have
made the pursuit of history a public phenomena and they have recognized and advanced the associated tourism benefits as an
internationally important social and economic force. From the latter
decades of the nineteenth century to the turn of the twentieth century, continually expanding efforts have been made to involve the
public in relevant historical process and understanding, and to im-
bue the attempts with high social and economic value. They have
been based on a timeless instinct to explain the present by reference
to the physical evidence of the past.

> Whether it is a natural instinct or a mere illusion, I can't
> say, but one's emotions are more strongly aroused by see-
> ing the places that . . . have been the favorite resort of
> men of note in former days, than by hearing about their
> deeds or reading their writings.[6]

When the Roman, Cicero, uttered these words more than two
thousand years ago he was surrounded by inspiring monuments to
civilization, many of which have survived as ruins and restorations
to this modern era. Neither the Louisbourg reconstruction with its
surrounding ruins nor the other historic sites and outdoor museums
reviewed in this book are likely to rival ancient Rome or its extant
remains as international historical monuments, and certainly not as
major tourist attractions. But Louisbourg and these other institutions do stand as important testimony to the historical preservation
movement and to the labors of research; serving both as a cultural

---

6   As quoted in Edward Alexander, "A Fourth Dimension for History
    Museums", *Curator*, Vol. 11, No. 4, 1968, p. 263.

legacy and as tourist attractions with high standards and, in at least Louisbourg's case, equally high potential. As Cicero entreated with respect to Rome and countless historians and museum commentators have preached and practiced since, Louisbourg and other outdoor museums and historic sites must be visited to be fully appreciated. As Edward Alexander has so often and eloquently pleaded in his writings, history is better experienced on location and in all of its dimensions.[7]

History is also better served and experienced when all classes of society are studied and when the monuments of ordinary folk are visited with the same enthusiasm as those of the rich and famous. Outdoor museums in general, especially folk museums in Europe and historical farms and historic sites in North America, are products of this century and in their presentations they have provided a balance to the elitist institutions and bourgeois historiography derived from the nineteenth century and earlier societies.

In its historical research programme and development as a historic site and outdoor museum, Louisbourg has taken special efforts not to perpetuate this tradition. This philosophy and policy evolved because the project developed during a period when most Canadian museums and cultural agencies enjoyed and actively sought general public support and involvement. A former Director of the Nova Scotia Museum, later President of the Canadian Museums Association and one of the earliest Canadian museologists to be named a fellow of the American Association of Museums, Donald K. Crowdis wrote in 1976 on the past and future development of Canadian museums:

> The biggest change in the last twenty-five or thirty years has been acceptance by the public. Several causes have been given — leisure, travel, the media, school involvement, a dif-

---

7   Ibid., pp. 263-289.

ferent attitude in museums. Whatever the cause, this public acceptance has changed our world.[8]

The process of stimulating thought by the visitor is characteristic of
systematic collecting, good curation and active interpretation. Ideas
form the essence of systematic collections, and the external world,
however perceived, gives rise to these ideas. Though collections in
history museums are both relics and reflections of the past, they are
explained in the present to a public that uses collections, their interpretations and their own intellect and personal experiences in an
attempt to understand both past and present.

> No one starts to form or to display a collection without
> inheriting past process, and each collection or display in
> place contributes its mite to the dynamics of change. The
> whole continuous reconstruction is part of the concrete
> appreciation of the world, with all its awkwardness and
> dislocation, and each actor in the story can be involved in
> the struggle.[9]

Pearce has articulated the compelling link between history and
the public, founded on the fundamental need within people to situ-
ate themselves in an often confusing world. This need to seek a
personal and public history through souvenirs and museum collections has been intensified in the post-industrial age, with its
dislocations and seemingly discontinuous change. We seem to need
history more than ever.

The pursuits of history work better in combination than in isolation, especially when they are intended for public consumption. The

---

8   Donald Crowdis, "Development of Canadian Museums", *Conference
    Proceedings for 2001: The Museum and the Canadian Public*, Ottawa,
    Canadian Museums Association, 1977, p.7.

9   Ibid., p. 150.

special communicative and richness of museums such as Louisbourg should be further acknowledged by educators and put to use by all who seek to further an understanding of the past, including academics, if the public is to benefit fully. The process of investigating meanings does not end with curators, museologists and historians, not even with museum educators and public historians, for the museum visitors — the public consumers of history — invest their own personal history, as they see fit, to derive impressions and understanding. It could be argued that every visit to a museum or historic site or, for that matter, every reading of a history text or viewing of a display or interpretation activity could produce a different set of experiences, perspectives and conclusions. This invested meaning can be altered by the museum or historic site experience, of course, but it is always a factor in the learning process, just as reading a book for the second time can produce different insights because we bring a different knowledge base to our comprehension of the original.

In a book of essays on *The New Museology* Ludmilla Jordanova, an historian at the University of Essex, offers an important commentary on the Jorvick Viking Centre in York that could be applied to the Louisbourg project and many other outdoor museums:

> . . . the claim is not simply that the museum generates knowledge, but rather that a simulacrum of the past is available that renders the conventional notion of a museum obsolete. The search for the authentic is taken to its limits, by stimulating *three* (author's italics) senses, and by stressing the ability not to convey information but to mimic experience . . .

> . . . many aspects of life cannot be conveyed through looking, smelling and listening — work, hunger, disease, war, death are obvious examples. We understand the past, not by spuriously re-experiencing it, but by turning over many different kinds of evidence relating to it and by generating from this an understanding which inevitably has a strong intellectual, that is, abstract component.[11]

Louisbourg and Public History

> From the rich sources that survive to record the half-cen-
> tury of this small, lively community on the Atlantic shore
> of Canada, we can discover how some ordinary people lived
> and died in eighteenth-century Canada, how they dressed
> and ate and built their homes, how they earned a living
> and raised their children, how they fell in love and went
> to war . . . since history usually denies us the chance to go
> past kings and heroes to the lives of the ordinary and the
> undistinguished, those rare occasions when we can make
> some ordinary people briefly famous are worth seizing.[10]

When former Louisbourg staff historian Christopher Moore wrote those words in 1982 the Louisbourg reconstruction project was nearing completion and receiving national acclaim from authors such as Moore, who had developed his approach to popular history as a staff historian at Louisbourg, and from increasing numbers of the general public who had developed a new sense of history from visits to the site, from reading about it and from thinking about its special relevance in their own lives. For more than two decades Louisbourg had developed as a mirror of Canadian heritage, reflecting French, English, Mi'kmaq and American traditions. It has also served as a testimony to the growth and maturity of the heritage preservation movement in Canada and to the vicissitudes of the Cape Breton economy. This dual impetus to commemorate a national monument and to stimulate the local economy had justified a level of human effort and financial expenditure that is not likely to be duplicated in Canada with such intensity over such a relatively short period of research and development.

The Louisbourg reconstruction, therefore, must be understood not only as a product of history and of this generation, but as an in-

---

10 Christopher Moore, *Louisbourg Portraits: Life in an Eighteenth-
Century Garrison Town*, Macmillan, Toronto, 1982, p. vii-viii.

ternationally important heritage centre and tourism product for future generations; an enduring commodity for public consumption in the cultural tourism marketplace. Ephemeral in the historical sense, Louisbourg now faces the challenge of relative permanency, subject not just to the ebb and flow of historical events and trends but to the uncertainties of current socio-economic and political forces and to the constraints of geography and culture.

The socio-economic plight of Cape Breton is not likely to improve substantially in the foreseeable future, so the basic economic justification for expenditures at Louisbourg will remain. One of the few opportunities for the area's economic improvement, the expansion of tourism, further supports Louisbourg's role as a major heritage centre, but a serious effort has to be made to convince politicians that heritage preservation and quality interpretation standards are not only compatible with tourism, but integral to its growth and renewal. These elements of 'sustainable development', to adopt one of the catch all phrases of the 1990s, have to be presented convincingly to professional and business groups, to the public and to the politicians who determine resource allocation:

> In the next 25 years the challenge may centre on the preservation of the integrity of the island's culture by entering more definitely into the political arena . . . . This will entail a greater degree of involvement on the part of museologists, historians, and archivists working with the so-called grass roots.[11]

At Louisbourg there is precedent for this involvement. J.S. McLennan, the leading proponent of Louisbourg's designation as a National Historic Site, worked regularly with prominent politicians and in later life became a member of the Canadian Senate. John

---

11   Robert J. Morgan, "The Heritage Movement in Cape Breton: Cultural integrity must not be lost in the scramble to lure tourist dollars", *The Forerunner* (Spring, 1988), p.7.

Lunn, the first Park Superintendent at the Louisbourg project and the prime mover for its research and development phase, regularly informed and courted politicians throughout his tenure at Louisbourg. This activity must continue if Louisbourg is to play a leading role as a heritage centre and an economic impetus to tourism in Cape Breton and Atlantic Canada.

The geographical and cultural constraints to expansion of Louisbourg's role as a heritage centre can be overcome. The site's geographical isolation on the southeast coast of Cape Breton is not a major obstacle in today's world of modern transportation and electronic information exchange. But the lack of a close socio-cultural identity between Louisbourg and the rest of Cape Breton Island remains: "The gap between the far-off days of the 18th century French occupation of the island and 20th century, largely English-speaking Cape Breton was too wide to allow a personal identification with the project."[12]

The obvious and distinct architectural manifestations of the French presence at Louisbourg add a diversity to the cultural landscape that is observed, studied and widely appreciated by Cape Bretoners and tourists alike, but there is a lack of direct historical and cultural identification with the historic site and its reconstruction. The proprietary interests of the industrial area residents and their political representatives need to be further developed over the next decade of consolidation and growth in cultural tourism and economy.

Louisbourg challenges its visitors and those who study it through other media to view Cape Breton and Canada, today and in history, in a different way. Its combination of natural and historical resources and blend of French, Mi'kmaq, British and New England traditions, impart a special educational opportunity; one of clear, provocative and instructive contrast with its surroundings. All that remains is to place the Louisbourg project, through high quality and sustainable educational and extension programming, on the map of

12 Ibid., p. 5.

international heritage preservation and tourism; a status achieved only in the course of time and always in cooperation with other heritage-related institutions and economic development agencies.

Conclusion:
Louisbourg Heritage

The report of the Rand Royal Commission in 1960 had marked a major turning point in the difficult evolution of the Cape Breton economy, and its observations and conclusions concerning Louisbourg provided a needed and welcome catalyst for the outdoor museum and historic site preservation movement and for public history in Canada. Its recommendation to partially reconstruct the eighteenth century ruins of Louisbourg resulted in the most ambitious heritage reconstruction project in the country, and eventually led to the creation of what became an international model for historic site preservation, interpretation and public history. In its role as an outdoor museum and tourist attraction, Louisbourg has further advanced the profile of public history in Canada and affirmed its impact on the tourism economy.

The human and financial resources allocated to the project were generous and the rich historical and archaeological record was very quickly recognized and exploited. It is doubtful that such progress could have been made without the availability of extensive international archival and museum collections and expertise, particularly from France, England and the United States, where source material was gathered and more experienced research staff and consultants were recruited. Though Canadian in purpose and design, the Louisbourg project had to be launched and sustained as an international effort.

Research and reconstruction methods became innovative and interdisciplinary, and control over standards and scheduling at the project passed from engineers and managers to design teams and committees. The level of participation by historians and archaeologists in every facet of the project from technical analysis to major decision making, planning and development was extremely high and came to characterize the research and development phase at Louisbourg.

The success of this interdisciplinary, methodological process coincided with growing public interest in the Louisbourg project and Canadian heritage preservation in general. In the years preceding and following Canadian centennial celebrations in 1967, the public history profile of the Louisbourg reconstruction as well as the popular appeal of its concurrent operation as a national historic site increased steadily. Within Parks Canada the project became both a model for historic site development and a significant drain on scarce resources. The socio-economic justifications for the project remained, however, and the additional tourism benefits and potential were increasingly recognized and expounded as a politically expedient rationale for continuing the research and development as well as operational programmes at a very high level of resource allocation throughout the 1970s.

High standards, generous resources, political support and public acceptance sustained momentum at the project through the difficult early years and through two decades of extensive research and development. With progress in its interpretation and visitor service programming, the Louisbourg project has found its place as one of the leading outdoor museums and historic sites in North America, comparable to some of the long established museum and cultural institutions of western Europe. The difficulties and limitations of the project, as well as its progress and achievements, essentially the lessons of the project as a model for historical preservation, interpretation and public history, can be summarized as follows.

Early Research and Source Gathering

The extent of the historical and archaeological record concerning Louisbourg determined the parameters and the primary objectives of the project brief. Though initially daunting to research and development staff, that data base, a clear legacy of the prominent French, British and American roles in the eighteenth century colonies of Isle Royale and Cape Breton, became an enduring and inspirational beacon for the project. The high research standards to which Parks Canada was committed allowed a very high degree of accuracy in reconstruction, a precedent and standard which became an imperative throughout research and development and which prevented the project from becoming just another historical recreation and tourist attraction. The extent and richness of data also confirmed the historical significance of Louisbourg in North American and European terms, and was a constant inspiration to project staff and ultimately to the Canadian public. The historical and the equally extensive archaeological records gathered in the first several years began to guide and to validate the reconstruction and its interpretation to the public.

Planning and the Role of Research

There was no formalized and systematic planning process for the Louisbourg project until its second decade of research and development, a deficiency that exacerbated serious research and reconstruction coordination and scheduling problems in the early years. Five-year capital forecasts prepared each year were an inadequate substitute. Philosophy and policy statements were available from Parks Canada to provide general direction, but the early years of resource allocation and practical project planning were fraught with professional conflict and scheduling difficulties. Many of these problems could have been avoided if the project had been preceded by a proper and sophisticated planning process, with sufficient research lead-time to stay well ahead of construction activity. This experience provided a valuable lesson for Parks Canada and helped to rationalize an extensive systems planning exercise with formal planning stages for major projects initiated after 1970.

Many of the mistakes made in resource allocation and scheduling were eventually overcome because of the high level of funding and expertise available to the project and because a solid teamwork ethic emerged at the Louisbourg site. After the first targets for reconstruction of the Kings Bastion were met in the late 1960s, a separate Parks Canada task force planning process for Louisbourg produced a set of 1973 planning documents to guide further research and development, including interpretation and public history programming. The 1973 task force planning documents also set the basic parameters for Louisbourg's operation as an outdoor museum and historic site.

Programming and Interdisciplinary Work

The teamwork ethic and practices developed at the Louisbourg project in the early 1960s were later formalized in a network of interdisciplinary teams and committees and integrated with the regular park organization to provide a complex but workable approach to programme development. That system became the most distinguishing feature of the Louisbourg research and development process, was emulated within Parks Canada and elsewhere in the Canadian historic site development field, and was further and formally entrenched at Louisbourg as a method of renewing and updating operational programmes.

The system of design teams and committees was essential in bringing the various disciplines together to resolve the sometimes conflicting research evidence and to work out other reconstruction problems. Interdisciplinarity was also a key element in developing a comprehensive range of interpretation themes and objectives as a basis for interpretation and public history programmes.

Reconstruction and Interpretation

In addition to the exchange of information within the team and committee system, a number of memoranda, reports and publications were prepared as part of the research and development process. From an early emphasis on structural, technical and military topics these manuscripts evolved to cover a range of social history subjects. The collection reflects the vast extent of historical evidence available, the changing pattern of reconstruction and interpretation over two decades, and the increasing sophistication and appeal of public history methods and products. The results have also altered the historiography of Isle Royale and New France in general and added significantly to Canadian academic and popular history.

Collectively the reports and publications provide an excellent foundation and starting point for additional interpretive and educational presentations in text, illustration, film and multimedia. Retention of the project archives and library as well as the vast archaeological research collections at Louisbourg after the completion of research and development has allowed Parks Canada to refine programmes at Louisbourg and its other historic sites; and to serve as a major resource centre for eighteenth century studies, historic site development and outdoos museum operation.

Museum programmes, of course, have similarly reflected the research and development process, but they also reflect new and formative experience at the operational level. The requirement to simultaneously interpret the Louisbourg site and to provide visitor services while the reconstruction progressed, combined with the inclusion of operations staff in the interdisciplinary system of teams and committees, have allowed a balance of traditional and innovative methods of exhibition and presentation. Interpretation methods such as costumed animation scenarios, candlelight tours, and the theme lounges that combine period appearance with modern comforts and communication technology, have been successfully tested and developed. In interpretation terms these are secondary to the reconstruction of original features and the presentation of reconstructed properties in combination with costumed animation, but these newer programmes have added to the balance of old and new interpretation methods.

Outdoor Museums and Historic Sites

Comparison of Louisbourg to other major outdoor museums and historic sites reveal patterns of research and development that have changed over the past century on the basis of national culture, institutional mandate and museological method. These comparisons suggest new directions for the Louisbourg project, principally in the entertainment and modern service components of interpretive, visitor service and educational programming. Comparisons have also underlined the paramount importance of preserving and developing Louisbourg as the original site of the eighteenth century fortress, town and harbour. The nature and impact of its interpretation and public history presentations is based on this quality, which distinguishes the Louisbourg site from many other historic sites and outdoor museums in the western world.

Public History

The Louisbourg project has developed beyond limited historic preservation to present a major case study in history making for the public. In addition to being a major outdoor museum and historic site the Louisbourg reconstruction functions as a set for historical scholarship and fiction, a public history prototype for the popularization of museums and living history. Its original historic resources, the high standards of research and development and its status as a national monument transcend popular theme parks in terms of historical depth and validity, but the site can actually rival such derivatives as a setting for books and films. Louisbourg's isolation from major and modern urban developments has provided historical and psychological contrast with the modern age, which has allowed the project to experiment more intensely with history making or living history programmes. Once again, the main potential in this area lies in Parks Canada's careful cooperation with outside agencies who can take full advantage of a properly managed collection of historical resources; without threatening their preservation.

There have been good books of scholarship and fiction written about Louisbourg, and films set within the reconstruction have progressed from early documentaries to a major Disney production during the spring and summer of 1993. Potential in these areas of history making will be further realized as international awareness of the Louisbourg project spreads and experience is gained in balancing these activities with existing preservation and interpretation programming. This potential is based on the sometimes profound intellectual and psychological impact of significant historical places and collections in general, accentuated at Louisbourg by the nature of its military and social history and its modern isolation. It is also based on the increasing mass appeal of public history.

Louisbourg represents the considerable heritage efforts of one generation of Canadians, with significant help from France, England and the United States. It has played a small but important role in history making and nation building and in the process it has set high and enduring research and development standards for future generations of public history adherents. The Louisbourg project is likely to contribute even more substantially in the future to the development of world heritage sites and to our own individual and collective sense of time and place in the history of civilization in the modern world.

Select
Bibliography

Notes on Primary Sources

Reference is required here to chapter one of this study, which provides an analysis of the extensive primary data base for research and development at Louisbourg.

General Inventory of Archival Holdings. Compiled by Paul Rose. 1970.
Louisbourg Map Collection. Compiled by Eric Krause. 1976.
Selection Lists for Archival Sources concerning Louisbourg and Cape Breton in the Public Records Office, London. Manuscript Report Series Nos. 137-41. Ottawa. Parks Canada. 1972.
Master List of In-house Reports Produced by, for and about the Fortress of Louisbourg and Related Sites. Compiled by Eric Krause. 1980.
The Fortress of Louisbourg General Inventory of Archival Holdings. Compiled by Eric Krause and Margaret Cameron. 1981. Revised 1983.
Fortress of Louisbourg Library: Guide and Brief Location Description. Compiled by Eric Krause et al. Search date 1989. (This is a computerized listing of library holdings, including the extensive project files which have served as an important primary source for this study.)

Secondary Sources (unpublished)

Portfolios of unpublished books, brochures, pamphlets, information sheets and press releases, maps, posters, postcards, photographs and slides have been compiled for the following museums and historic sites visited during the research phase of this study:

Alexander Graham Bell Museum, Baddeck, Nova Scotia

Art Gallery of Ontario, Toronto, Ontario

Banff National Park, Alberta

Beamish North of England Open Air Museum

Belgrave Hall, Leicester

Berwick-Upon-Tweed Fortifications

Biological Museum, Djurgarden, Stockholm

Blists Hill Open Air Museum, Telford

Boston Childrens Museum, Boston, Massachussetts

Bosworth Field, Leicester

British Museum (Natural History), London

Canadian War Museum, Ottawa, Ontario

Cape Breton Centre for Heritage and Science, Sydney, Nova Scotia

Cape Breton Highlands National Park, Nova Scotia

Chichester Cathederal, West Sussex

Coalbrookdale and The Museum of Iron, Telford

Colonial Williamsburg, Virginia

Department of Environment, Ancient Monuments (various sites)

Department of Environment, Parks Canada (various historic sites)

Hadrian's Wall, Northumberland

Halifax Defence Complex, Nova Scotia

Hotel Des Invalides, Paris

Ironbridge Gorge Museum Trust and the Iron Bridge, Telford

Kings Landing, New Brunswick

Leicestershire Museum, Leicester

Maritime Museum of the Atlantic, Halifax, Nova Scotia

McCord Museum, Montreal, Quebec

Miners Museum, Glace Bay, Nova Scotia
Musée de la Marine, Paris
Musée de l'Armee, Paris
Mystic Seaport, Connecticut
National Maritime Mueum, Greenwich, London
National Museum of Man (Civilization), Ottawa, Ontario
National Museum (Natural Sciences), Ottawa, Ontario
National Museum of Technology, Ottawa, Ontario
National Trust for Britain (various properties)
New Brunswick Museum, St. John, New Brunswick
Nova Scotia Museum, Halifax, Nova Scotia
Old Sturbridge Village, Massachussetts
Old Fort Henry, Kingston, Ontario
Plimouth Plantation, Massachusetts
Portsmouth and Southampton Harbour Defences, Hampshire
Royal Ontario Museum, Toronto, Ontario
Rutland Water Nature Resrve, Leicester
Skansen Open Air Museum, Stockholm
St. Helen's Island Fortifications, Montreal, Quebec
Tower of London
Upper Canada Village, Cornwall, Ontario
Warwick Castle
Weald and Downland Open Air Museum, Singleton, Sussex

Publications

Adams, B. "The Construction and Occupation of the Barracks of the King's Bastion at Louisbourg". *Occasional Papers in Archaeology and History No. 18*. Ottawa. Parks Canada. 1978.

Alderson, William T. "The Objectives of Historic Site Preservation". *Museum*. Vol. XXVII. No. 3. 1975.

Alderson, William T. and Low, Shirley P. *Interpretation of Historic Sites*. Nashville, Tennessee. American Association for State and Local History. 1976.

Alexander, Edward P. "A Fourth Dimension for History Museums". *Curator*. Vol. 11. No. 4. 1968.

Alexander, Edward P. "An Orientation Program for Colonial Williamsburg". *Museum News*. Vol. 26. No. 20. 1949.

Alexander, Edward P. "Artistic and Historical Period Rooms". Curator. Vol. 7. No. 4. 1964.

Alexander, Edward P. "Bringing History to Life." *Curator*. Vol. 4. No. 1. 1961.

Alexander, Edward P. *Museum Masters: Their Museums and Their Influence*. Nashville. American Association for State and Local History. 1984.

Alexander, Edward P. *Museums in Motion*. Nashville, Tennessee. American Association for State and Local History. 1979.

Alexander, Edward P. "Our British Cousins and their Museums". *Curator*. Vol. 5. No. 2. 1962.

Alexander, Edward P. *The Interpretation Philosophy of Colonial Williamsburg*. Williamsburg. Colonial Wiliamsburg Foundation. 1971.

Allan et al. "Display Policy in Museums: A Symposium". Proceedings of British Museums Association Annual Conference, 1961. *Museums Journal*. Vol. 61. No. 3. Dec. 1961.

Alt, M.B. "Improving Audio-visual Presentations". *Curator*. Vol. 22. No. 2. 1975.

Anderson, Jay. *Time Machines: The World of Living History*. Nashville, Tennessee. The American Association for State and Local History. 1984.

Angotti, Thomas. "Planning the Open-air Museum and Teaching Urban History: the United States in the World Context". *Museum*. Vol. XXXIV. No. 3. 1982.

Anonymous. *The Great Importance of Cape Breton, Demonstrated and Exemplified, by Extracts from the best Writers, French and English, who have treated of that Colony*. London. John Brindley. 1746.

Anthony, Robert N. and Herzlinger, Regina. *Management Control in Nonprofit Organizaations*. Homewood, Illinois. Richard. D. Irwin. 1975.

Armstrong, J.R. and Harris, R. *Weald and Downland Open Air Museum Singleton: Main Guide*. Worthing, Sussex. Weald and Downland Open Air Museum. 1977.

Arsenault, Bona. *Louisbourg, 1713-1758*. Quebec. Le Conseil de la Vie francaise en Amerique. 1971.

Atkinson, Frank and Holton, Michael. "Open Air and Folk Museums". *Museums Journal*. Vol. 72. No. 4. March, 1973.

Baehrendtz, Nils, Erik et al. "From one Museum to Another: Skansen-a Stock Taking at Ninety". *Museum*. Vol. 36. No. 3. 1982.

Bacon, R. "Folklife and the American Museum". *Museum News*. Vol. 59. No. 5. 1981.

Baker, Raymond F. "A Campaign of Amateurs: The Siege of Louisbourg." *Occasional Papers in Archaeology and History No. 18*. Ottawa. Parks Canada. 1978.

Balcom, B.A. "New Englanders Take Louisbourg, 1745". *Cape Breton's Magazine*. No. 19. 1978.

Balcom, B.A. "The Cod Fishery of Isle Royale, 1713-58". *Studies in Archaeology, Architecture and History No. 13*. Ottawa. Parks Canada. 1984.

Barnes, Frank. "Viewpoint: Living History, Clio or Cliopatra". *History News*. Vol. 29. No. 9. 1974.

Barr, D.. "Interpretive Textual Material" . *Communicating With the Museum Visitor*. Toronto. Royal Ontario Museum. 1976.

Bayle, Luc-Marie and Mordal, Jacques. *Le Musee de la Marine*. Paris. Ouest-France. 1980.

Beam, Kenneth. "Marketing the Museum". *Musum News*. Ja./Feb. 1979.

Beardsley, Donald C. "Helping Teachers to Use Museums". *Curator*. Vol. 18. No. 3. 1975.

Belcher, M. "The Role of the Designer in the Museum". *Museums Journal*. Vol. 70. No. 2. 1970.

Benedict, Paul. "Historic Site Interpretation: The Student Field Trip." *History News*. Vol. 26. No. 3. 1971.

Benes, Josef. "Audio-Visual Media in Museums". *Museum*. Vol. XXVIII. No. 2. 1976.

Bennett, Peter H. "Furniture for History". *Canadian Antiques Collector*. Vol. 4. No. 11. 1969.

Black, C.C. "The Case for Research". *Museum News*. Vol. 58. No. 5. 1980.

Blanchard, Kenneth. *The One Minute Manager*. New York. Berkeley Books. 1981.

Bourinot, John. *Historical and Descriptive Account of the Island of Cape Breton and of Its Memorials of the French Regime*. Montreal. Foster and Brown. 1892.

Bosher, J.F. *The Canada Merchants 1713 — 1763*. Oxford: Clarendon Press. 1987.

British Tourist Authority, *Museum Lessons from the USA*. London. British Tourist Authority. 1983.

Brown, Martyn. "One Museum's Drama Experience". *Museums Journal*. Vol. 81. No. 4. March, 1982.

Brown, Richard. *A History of the Island of Cape Breton*. London. Sampson, Low, Son, and Marston. 1869.

Burage, Henry S. *Maine at Louisbourg in 1745*. Augusta, Maine. Burleigh and Flynt. 1910.

Burcaw, G. Ellis. "Can History Be too Lively?". *Museums Journal*. Vol. 80. No. 1. June, 1980.

Burcaw, G. Ellis. *Introduction to Museum Work*. Nashville, Tennessee. American Association for State and Local History. 1975.

Cameron, D.F. "A Viewpoint: the Museum as a Communications System and Implications for Museum Education". *Curator*. Vol.11, No. I (1968).

Cameron, D.F. "How Do We Know What Our Visitors Think?" *Museum News*. Vol. 45. No. 7. 1967.

Cameron, D.F. "Measuring Effectiveness: The Evaluator's Viewpoint". *Museum News*. Vol. 46. No. 5. 1968.

Cameron, D.F. "The Creative Audience". *The Museologist*. No. 114. 1970.

Cameron, D.F. "The Museum: A Temple of the Forum". *Curator*. Vol. 14. No. 1. 1971.

Canada Year Book, 1961. Ottawa. Dominion Bureau of Statistics. 1961.

Canadian Historical Association. *Papers and Abstracts for a Symposium on Isle Royale During the French Regime*. Ottawa. National Museums of Canada. 1972.

Canadian Museums Association. *A Guide to Museum Positions Including a Statement on the Ethical Behavior of Museum Professionals*. Ottawa. Canadian Museums Association. 1979.

Canadian Museums Association. "Marketing and Museums: Special Theme Issue". *Muse*. Summer. 1986.

Canadian Museums Asociation and National Museums of Canada. *Economic Impacts of Heritage Institutions on the Canadian Economy: Analysis of Methods; Statistical Digest*. Ottawa. Canadian Museums Association. 1985.

Cape Breton County Economic Development Authority. *Strategic Economic Development Plan*. Sydney. Nova Scotia, August, 1994.

Caplan, Ron (ed.). "New Englanders Take Louisbourg, 1745. A Narrative of the First Seige, with Extracts from French and English Diaries." Wreck Cove. *Cape Breton's Magazine*. 1988.

Capstick, Brenda. "Museums and Tourism". *The International Journal of Museum Management and Curatorship*. Vol. 4. 1985.

Chambers, M. "Is Anyone Out There? Audience and Commuication". *Museum News*. Vol. 62. No. 5. 1984.

Chenhall, R.G. *Nomenclature for Museum Cataloguing: A System for Classifying Man-Made Objects*. Nashville, Tennessee. American Association for State and Local History. 1978.

Clark, Andrew Hill. *Acadia: The Geography of Early Nova Scotia to 1760*. Madison. University of Wisconsin. 1968.

Clark, Andrew Hill. "New England's Role in the Underdevelopment of Cape Breton Island during the French Regime". *Canadian Geographer*. Vol. 9. No. 1. 1965

Clark, Gregory. *Royal Naval Museum*. Aldershot, Hants. Wellington Press. n.d.

Clavell, James. *Gai-Jin: A Novel of Japan*. New York. Delacorte Press. 1993.

Cohen, Allan R. *Effective Behavior n Organzations: Learning from the Interplay of Cases, Concepts and Student Experiences*, Homewood, Ill., R.D. Irwin. 1980.

Colonial Williamsburg. *Official Guidebook and Map*. Wiliamsburg, Virginia. Colonial Williamsburg Foundation. 1976.

Cossons, Neil. "The Conservation of Industrial Monuments". *Museums Journal*. Vol. 74. No. 2. (Sept., 1974).

Cossons, Neil. "The Ironbridge Project". *Museums Journal*. Vol. 72. No. 4. March, 1973.

Cossons, Neil (ed.). *The Management of Change in Museums*. Greenwich. National Martime Museum. 1985.

Cossons, Neil. "The Museum in the Valley, Ironbridge Gorge". *Museum*. Vol. xxxii. No. 3. 1980.

Cossons, Neil and Trinder, Barrie. *The Iron Bridge: Symbol of the Industrial Revolution*. Wiltshire. Ironbridge Gorge Museum Trust and Moonraker Press. 1979.

Cossons, Neil. "The New Museum Movement in the United Kingdom". Museum. No. 138 (Vol. XXXV, No. 2). 1983.

Countryside Commission. *Interpretive Media and Facilities*. Edinburg. HMSO for Countryside Commission. 1975.

Countryside Commission. *Interpretive Planning*. Cheltenham. Countryside Commission.1977. revised 1979.

Countryside Commission. *Interpretation in Visitor Centres*. Cheltenham. Countryside Commission . 1978.

Countryside Commission. *Audio-Visual Media in Countryside Interpretation*. Countryside Commission. Cheltenham.1980.

Cramer, Ted and Beam, Kenneth. "Marketing the Museum". *Museum News*. Vol. 57. No. 3. 1979.

Crepeau, Andree. "An Inventory of People Working on the Material Culture of Eighteenth-Century Louisbourg". *Material History Bulletin No. 18*. 1983.

Crowdis, Donald K. "Development of Canadian Museums". *Conference Proceedings for 2001: The Museum and the Canadian Public*. Ottawa. Canadian Museums Association. 1977.

Crowley, Terry. "The Inroads of Secularization in Eighteenth-Century New France: church and people at Louisbourg". *Historical Studies*. Toronto. Canadian Catholic Historical Association. 1984.

Cummings, L.L. and Kirby, Warren. *Effective Behavior in Organizations: Learning From the Interplay of Cases, Concepts and Student Experiences*. Homewood, Illinois. Richard D. Irwin. 1984.

Dalibard, Jacques. "Starting Another Century: More than Ever, We Need Parks Canada Leadership." Ottawa. *Canadian Heritage*. May/June. 1985.

Dartington Amenity Research Trust. *Defence of the Realm: an Interpretive Strategy for Portsmouth and the surrounding region*. Devon. Dartington Amenity Research Trust. 1979.

DeForest, L.E. *Louisbourg Journals 1745*. New York. Society for Colonial Wars in the State of New York. 1932.

Deparment of Environment. *Official Handbooks: Caernarfon Castle and Town Walls, Corbridge Roman Station, Fortifications of Berwick-Upon Tweed, Housesteads Roman Fort, North Wales Quarrying Museum, Stonehenge*. London. HMSO. 1952-75.

Department of the Environment, Scottish Development Department. *List and Map of Historic Monuments Open to the Public*. London. HSMO. 1972.

Department of Environment. *Stonehenge and Avebury*. London. HSMO. 1959.

Department of Environment. *Tower of London Official Guide*. London. HMSO. 1981.

Dickason, Olive Patricia. "Louisbourg and the Indians: A Study in Imperial Race Relations, 1713-1760". *History and Archaeology No. 6*. Ottawa. Parks Canada. 1976.

Dictionary of Canadian Biography. Vol. 1, 1000-1700. Vol. 11, 1701-1740. Vol. 111, 1741-1770. Toronto. University of Toronro Press. 1969-1974.

Dixon, Brian, et al. *The Museum and the Canadian Public*. Ottawa. Arts and Culture Branch. 1974.

Donovan, Kenneth (ed.). *Cape Breton at 200; historical essays in honor of the Island's bicentennial, 1785 — 1985*. Sydney. University College of Cape Breton Press. 1985.

Donovan, Kenneth. "Communities and Families: Family Life and Living Conditions in Eighteenth Century Louisbourg" . *Material History Bulletin, No. 15*, Ottawa. National Museum of Man. 1979.

Donovan, Kenneth. "Family Life in 18th Century Louisbourg". *Manuscript Report No. 271*. Ottawa. Parks Canada. 1977.

Donovan, Kenneth. "Ile Royale, 18th Century." *Historical Atlas of Canada,* From the Beginning to 1800. Toronto. University of Toronto Press. 1987.

Donovan, Kenneth. "The Marquis de Chabert and the Louisbourg Observatory in the 1750's". *The American Neptune*. Vol. XLIV, No. 3. (Summer, 1984).

Downey, Fairfax. *Louisbourg: Key to a Continent*. Englewood Cliffs, New Jersey. Prentice-Hall. 1965.

Dunn, John. "The Louisbourg Lighthouse", "The Militia in Isle Royale". *Manuscript Report Series Nos. 32-33*. Ottawa. Parks Canada. 1971

Dunton, Hope. *From the Hearth: Recipes from the World of 18th-century Louisbourg*. Sydney. University College of Cape Breton Press. 1986.

Dunton, John. "Building Hardware Excavated at the Fortress of Louisbourg". *Manuscript Report Number 97*. Ottawa. Parks Canada. 1972.

Edwards. Yorke. "The Unatural Natural History in Museums". *Canadian Museums Association Gazette*. Vol. 12. No. 2. 1974.

Embleton, Ronald and Daniels, Charles. *Hadrian's Wall Reconstructed*. Newcastle upon Tyne. Frank Graham. 1981.

Emery-Wallis, F.A.J.. "The Value of Museums to the Economy". *Museums Journal*. Vol. 79. No. 3. Dec., 1979.

Encyclopedie ou Dictionnaire Rasionne des Sciences, des Arts et des Metiers, par une Societe de Gens de Lettres. 17 vols. Paris. Briasson. 1751-1752; *Supplement a Encyclopedie*. 4 Vols. 1777.

English Tourist Board Socio-Economic Research Unit. *Interpretive Techniques at Historic Buildings: Visitor Use and Reaction*. London. English Tourist Board. 1982.

Fairley, J. *History Teaching through Museums*. London. Longmans. 1977.

Farnell, G. "Team Briefing: A Means of Improving Communication within the Museum". *International Journal of Museum Management and Curatorship*. Vol. 3. No.2. 1984.

Fennely, Catherine. *Old Sturbridge Village*. Williamsburg, Virginia. Walter H. Miller. 1964.

Finlay, Greg. "The Museum and the Historian: Towards a New Partnership". *Canadian Museums Association Gazette*. Spring. 1978.

Fortier, John and Fitzgerald, Owen. *Fortress of Louisbourg*. Toronto. Oxford University Press. 1979.

Fortier, John. "The Fortress of Louisbourg and Its Cartographic Collection". *Association For Preservation Technology*, Vol. 4. Nos. 1-2. Havertown, Pennsylvania. Association For Preservation Technology. 1972.

Fortier, John. *Training for Interpretive Staff, Fortress of Louisbourg National Historic Park*. Louisbourg. Parks Canada. 1973.

Fortier, John. "What to do After the Architect Leaves". *Gazette*. Vol. 9. No.2. 1976.

Fortier, Margaret. "The Cultural Landscape of 18th Century Louisbourg". *Microfiche Report Series No. 83*. Ottawa. Parks Canada. 1983.

Fortier, Margaret. "The Isle Royale Garrison, 1713-45". *Microfiche Report Series No. 67*. Ottawa. Parks Canada. 1981.

Fortress of Louisbourg National Historic Park. *A Louisbourg Primer*. Louisbourg. Parks Canada. 1981.

Fortress of Lousbourg National Historic Park. *1977 Park Visitor Survey* (Preliminary). Louisbourg. Parks Canada. April 1978.

Foster, Richard. "The Changing Philosophy of Museums". *Museums Journal*. Vol. 79. No. 2. (Sept.,1979).

Foster, Wayne. *Post-Occupational History of the Old French Town of Louisbourg 1760-1930*. Louisbourg. Fortress of Louisbourg. 1965.

Frankland, Noble. "Military Museums Beyond the Barrack Wall". *Museums Journal*. Vo. 75. No. 3. 1975.

Fry, W. Bruce. "An Appearance of Strength: The Fortifications of Louisbourg". *Studies in Archaeology, Architecture and History*. Ottawa. Parks Canada. 1984.

Frye, L. Thomas. "The Recent Past is Prologue". *Museum News*. Vol. 55. No. 3. 1974.

Gailber, M. "Cooperation within Museum Walls: The Team Approach to Exhibition Development". *Museum Studies Journal*. Vol. 1. No. 3. 1984.

Galt, George. "Making History: a reconstructed eighteenth-century stands as a symbol of our confusion about what history is truly Canadian, and how to possess it." *Saturday Night*. Vol. 102. No. 1. (January, 1987).

Greenhill, Basil G.. *Guide to National Maritime Museum: Greenwich*. London. HMSO. 1981.

Greenhill, Basil(ed.). *The National Maritime Museum*. London. Philip Wilson Publishers Ltd. and Summerfield Press Ltd.. 1982.

Greer, Allan. "The Soldiers of Isle Royale, 1720-45." *History and Archaeology No. 28*. Ottawa. Parks Canada. 1979.

Gulbeck, P.E. *The Care of Historical Collections*. American Association for State and Local History. Nashville. 1972.

Guide to Canada's National Historic Parks. Ottawa. Parks Canada. 1982.

Guthe, Carl E. *The Management of Small History Museums*. Nashville, Tennessee. American Association for Statae and Local History. 1959.

Gwyn, Julian. "Shipbuilding for the Royal Navy in Colonial New England." *American Neptune*. Vol. XLVIII. No. 1. (Winter, 1988).

Gwyn, Julian. *The Royal Navy and North America: The Warren Papers, 1736-1752*. London. Navy Records Society. 1975.

Gwyn, Julian. "The Royal Navy in North America, 1712-1776". *The British Navy and the Use of Naval Power in the Eighteenth Century*. edited by Jeremy Black and Philip Woodfine. Leicester. Leicester University Press. 1988.

Gwyn, Julian and Moore, Christopher. *La Chute de Louisbourg: le journal du 1er siege de Louisbourg du 25 Mars au 17 juillet 1745 par Lacroix-Girard*. Ottawa. Editions de l'Universitie d'Ottawa. 1978.

Hale, John. "Museums and the Teaching of History". *Museum*. Vol. 21. No. 1. 1968.

Harrison, Richard. "The Need for a Collecting Pollicy". *Museums Journal*. Vol. 69. No. 3. (Dec.,1969).

Head of Visitor Resources Department of Public Services British Museum (Natural History). "Improving Audio-Visual Presentations". *Curator.* 22/2. 1979.

Hitsman, J. Mackay and Bond, C.C.J.. "Louisbourg: A Foredoomed Fortress". *Canadian Army Journal.* Vol. 10. No. 2. April, 1956.

Hitsman, J. Mackay with Bond, C.C.J. "The Assault Landing at Louisbourg, 1758". *Canadian Historical Review.* Vol. XXXV. No. 4. Dec. 1954.

Hobbley, Brian and Rylatt, Margaret. "The Lunt Roman Fort Museum and Interpretive Centre 1965-1974". *Museums Journal.* Vol. 74. No. 4. March, 1975.

Hogg, Gary. *Museums of England.* New York. Arco Publishing Company, Inc.. 1973.

Horne, Donald. *The Great Museum: The Re-Presentation of History.* London. Pluto Press. 1984.

Hudson, Kenneth. *A Social History of Museums.* London. Macmillan. 1975.

Hutchison, Rosemary. Furnishing the Fortress: Interpreting 1740's Households" *Canadian Collector*, Vol. 20. No. 2. 1985.

Ironbridge and Coalbrookdale Society. *Walks in the Severn Gorge.* Telford, Shropshire. Ironbridge and Coalbrookdale Society. 1984.

Ironbridge Gorge Museum. *Blists Hill Activity Guide.* Great Britain. Longmans. 1984.

Ironbridge Gorge Museum. *Museum Guides: Coalbrookdale Museum of Iron, Blists Hill Open Air Museum, The Iron Bridge, and Coalport China Works Museum.* Telford, Shropshire. IGMT. 1979.

Ironbridge Gorge Museum. *Teachers Handbook.* Telford, Shropshire. (IGMT). 1981.

Ironbridge Gorge Museum. *Visitor Survey Report* (conducted by Peter Nias, Research Surveys). Telford, Shropshire. IGMT. 1985

Johnston, A.J.B. "Before the Loyalists: Acadians in the Sydney Area, 1749-1754". *Cape Breton's Magazine.* No. 48. Wreck Cove. 1988.

Johnston, A.J.B. "Canada's First Lighthouse." The Atlantic Advocate. Vo. 76. No. 6. (February, 1986).

Johnston, A.J.B. "Lady Artists of Cape Breton. Louise Bradley McLennan and Hetty Donne Kimber". *Canadian Collector.* Vol. 21. No. 2 (March-April, 1986).

Johnston, A.J.B. *Religion in Life at Louisbourg 1713-1758*. Kingston, Ont. McGill-Queens University Press. 1984.

Johnston, A.J.B. "The People of Eighteenth-Century Louisbourg". *Nova Scotia Historical Quarterly/Review*. Vol. 11. No. 2. 1991.

Johnston, A.J.B. "Louisbourg: The Twists of Time." *The Beaver.* Vol. 316. No. 1. (Summer, 1985).

Johnston, A.J.B. "The Summer of 1744: A Portrait of Life in 18th-Century Louisbourg". *Studies in Archaeology, Architecture and History No. 4.* Ottawa. Parks Canada. 1984.

Kalman, Harold. *The Evaluation of Historic Buildings*. Ottawa. Parks Canada.1980.

Kavanagh, Gaynor. *History Curatorship*. Leicester. Leicester University Press. 1990.

Kay, W.K. *Keep It Alive: Tips on Living History Demonstrations*. Washington. National Parks Service. 1970.

Keck, Caroline K. et al. *A Primer on Museum Security*. Cooperstown, New York. New York State Historical Association. 1966.

Key, A. *Beyond Four Walls: The Origins and Development of Canadian Museums*. Toronto. McClleland and Stewart. 1973.

Kittleman, J.M. "Museum Mismanagement". *Museum News*. Vol. 54. No. 4. 1976.

Knez, E. I., & Wright, A. G.. "The Museum as a Communications System: an Assesment of Cameron's Viewpoint". *Curator*. Vol.13. No. 3 (1970).

Koppel, Peter. "Marketing Management and Museums". *Muse*. Summer. 1986.

Krause, Eric. "The Fortress of Louisbourg Archives: the first twenty-five years". *Archivaria*. No. 26. (Summer, 1988).

Larrabee, Edward McM. "Archaeological Research at the Fortress of Louisbourg". *Occasional Papers in Archaeology and History No. 2*. Ottawa. Parks Canada. 1971.

Larrabee, Edward McM. *Museums and Education*. Washington.
Smithsonian. 1968.

LeGoff, Tim. "Artillery at Louisbourg". *Manuscript Report No. 50*. Ottawa.
Parks Canada. 1967.

Lemieux, L. "Canadian Museums and their Role in Social Issues".
Curator. Vol. 14, No. 1. 1971.

"Le Musee Des Plans Reliefs". *Extrait de Cuilure et Communication. No. 21*.
Paris Ministere de la Communication. 1979.

Lewis, Ralph H. *A Manual for Museums*. Washington. Government
Printing Office. 1976.

Lewis, Ralph H. "Site Museums and National Parks". *Curator*. Vol. 11.
No. 2. 1959.

Lincoln, Crawford. "Museum Programs as Money Makers: The Old
Sturbridge Village Experience". *Curator*. Vol. 26. No. 1. 1983.

Lindsay, Charles S. "Louisbourg Guardhouses". *Occasional Papers in
Archaeology and History No. 12*. Ottawa. Parks Canada. 1975.

Lindsay, G.C. "Museums and Research in History and Technology".
Curator. Vol 5. No. 3. 1962.

Linn, Marcia C. "Exhibit Evaluation-Informed Decision Making".
Curator. Vol. 19. No. 4. 1976.

Lochan, K.A. "The Research Function as a Philosopher's Stone". *Muse*.
Vol. 16. No. 23. 1982.

Loomis, R.J. "Please, Not Another Visitor Survey" *Museum News*. Vol. 52.
No. 2. 1973.

Lowenthal, David. *The Past is a Foreign Country*. Cambridge University
Press. 1985.

Lowe, John. "The Weald and Downland Open Air Museum". *Museums
Journal*. Vol. 72. No. 1. (June, 1972).

Lunn, John. "Colonial Louisbourg and its Developing Ceramics
Collection". *Ceramics in America*. Charlottesville. University Press of
Virginia. 1973.

Lunn, John. "Louisbourg: the Forgotten Fortress". *Antiques*. June, 1970.

Lunn, John. "New Structures, New People, New Roles". *Conference
Proceedings for 2001: The Museum and the Canadian Public*. Ottawa.
Canadian Museums Association. 1977.

MacLean, Terrence D. "Block 4, Louisbourg, 1713-1768". *Manuscript Report Series No. 176*. Ottawa. Parks Canada. 1974.

MacLean, Terry. "Historical Research at Louisbourg: A Case Study in Museum Research and Development". in Donovan, Kennneth (ed.) *Cape Breton at 200: Essays in Honor of the Island's Bicentennial*. Sydney. University College of Cape Breton Press. 1985.

MacNutt, W.S. *The Atlantic Provinces: The Emergence of Colonial Society, 1712-1857*.Toronto. McClelland and Stewart. 1965.

Magi, Giovani. *Paris: Historical Outline and Photographs*. Paris. Florence. Bonechi. 1981.

Massey, Vincent. *Report of the Royal Commission on Arts, Letters and Sciences*. Ottawa. King's Printer. 1951.

McLennan, John Stewart. "Louisbourg". *Canadian Geographical Journal*. October, 1931.

McLennan, John Stewart. *Louisbourg from Its Foundation to its Fall, 1713-1758*. London. MacMillan. 1918.

McLuhan, Marshall. *Understanding Media: The Extensions of Man*. New York. New American Library. 1973.

McLuhan, Marshall et al. *Exploration of the Ways, Means, and Values of Museum Communication With the Viewing Public: A Seminar*. New York. Museum of the City of New York. 1969.

Ministry of Public Building and Works. *Ancient Monuments and Historic Buildings Open to the Public*. London. HMSO. 1968.

Miquelon, Dale. *New France 1701-1744. A Supplement to Europe*. Toronto. McClelland and Stewart. 1987.

Miquelon, Dale. "Canada's Place in the French Imperial Economy: An Eighteenth-Century Overview." *French Historical Studies*. Vol. 100. No. 3 (Spring, 1988).

Moore, Christopher and Sunderland, Terry. *Fortress of Louisbourg: Guide*. Sydney, Nova Scotia. Fortress of Louisbourg Volunteers Association and College of Cape Breton Press.

Moore, Christopher. "Commodity Imports of Louisbourg, Fortress of Louisbourg". *Manuscript Report Series No. 317*. Ottawa. Parks Canada. 1975.

Moore, Christopher. "How They Crossed the Ocean Accurately in 1753". *Canadian Geographic*. Vol. 101. No. 6. (December, 1981/January, 1982).

Moore, Christopher. *Louisbourg Portraits: Life in an Eighteenth-Century Garrison Town*. Toronto. Macmillan of Canada. 1982.

Moore, Christopher. "Place du Port" (1974), "Commodity Imports of Louisbourg" (1975), "Street Life and Public Activities in Louisbourg: Four Studies for Animators" (1978). *Manuscript Report Series No. 317*. Ottawa. Parks Canada. 1978.

Morgan, Robert J. "Block 16, Louisbourg, 1713-1768". *Manuscript Report Series No. 176*. Ottawa. Parks Canada. 1975.

Munro, Gordon. "Museum Shops From the Outside". *Museums Journal*. Vol. 76. No. 4. March, 1977.

Neal, A.. *Help! For the Small Museum*. Colorado. Pruett Publishing. 1969.

Neal, A.. *Exhibits for the Small Museum*. Nashville, Tennessee. American Association for State and Local History. 1976.

Noel Hume, Ivor. *A Guide to Artifacts of Colonial America*. New York. Alfred A. Knopf. 1970.

Nova Scotia, Department of Education. *Journal of Education* (special museums issue). Sixth Series. 1982.

Olson, James C. *The Role of Local History*. Nashville, Tennnessee. American Association for State and Local History. 1940.

Palardy, Jean. "Eighteenth Century French Faience in Canada". *Cahiers de la Ceramique, du Verre et des Arts du Feu*. Sevres. 48-9. 1971.

Palardy, Jean. "Reconstitution de l'ameublement de Louisbourg". *Vie des Arts*. Vol. 46. 1967.

Parkman, Francis. *A Half Century of Conflict*. Boston. Little, Brown. 1892.

Parks Canada, *Parks Canada Policy*. Ottawa. Parks Canada. 1979.

Parks, Roger and Sloat, Caroline(eds.). "Old Sturbridge Village". *Rural Visitor*. Sturbridge. Massachusetts. Friends of Old Sturbridge Village. 1980.

Parr, A.E. "Location, Motivation, and Duration of Museum Attendance". *Curator*. Vol. 10. No. 3. 1967.

Parr, A.E. "Marketing the Message". *Curator*. Vol. 12. No. 2. (1969).

Parr, A.E. "The Functions of Museums: Research Centres or Show Places". *Curator. Vol. 6. No. 1. 1963.*

Pearce, S.M. "The Role of the Archaeological Curator in the Wider Pattern of Archaeological Research: Some Suggestions". *Museums Journal*. Vol. 73. No. 4. 1974.

Pearce, S.M. *Museums, Objects and Collections: A Cultural Study* Leicester University Press. Leicester and London. 1992

Perrin, Richard. *Outdoor Museums*. Milwaukee. Milwaukee Public Museum. Publication in Museology No. 4. 1975.

Pichon, Thomas. *Genuine Letters and Memoirs, Relating to the Natural, Civil and Commercial History of the Islands of Cape Breton and Saint John*. London. J. Nourse. 1760.

Plumb, J.H. *England in the Eighteenth Century, 1714-1815*. Middlesex, England. Penguin. 1950.

Priestley, John. "An American Seminar on the Open Site Museum". *Museums Journal*. Vol. 73. No. 1. June, 1973.

Rabinowitz, Richard. "Museum Education at Old Sturbridge Village". *Museums' Annual: Education — Cultural Action*. Vol. 5. 1973.

Rand, I.C. *Report of the Royal Commission on Coal*. Ottawa. Queen's Printer. 1960.

Rawlyk, George. *Yankees at Louisbourg*. Orono, Maine. University of Maine. 1967.

Rider, Peter. E. *The History of Atlantic Canada: Museum Interpretations*. Ottawa. National Museum of Man. 1981.

Rider, Peter E. (ed.) *Studies in History and Museums*. Ottawa. Canadian Museum of Civilization. 1994.

Ripley, S. Dillon. "Museums and Education". *Curator*. Vol. 11. No. 3. 1968.

Rivers, Julian Pitt. "Reflections on the Concept of Museums and Interdisciplinarity". *Museum*. Vol. XXXII. No. 1/2. 1980.

Royal Ontario Museum. *Communicating With the Museum Visitor: Guidelines for Planning*. Toronto. Royal Ontario Museum. 1976.

Rutherfurd, Edward. *Sarum: The Novel of England*. London, Ballantine Books. 1987.

Sandwith, H. & Swainton, S. (eds.). *The National Trust Manual of Housekeeping*. London. Allen Lane. 1984.

Schettel, Harris H. "Exhibits: Art Form or Education Medium?" *Museum News*. Vol. 52. No. 1. 1973.

Schlebecker, J.T. "The Use of Objects in Historical Research". *Agricultural History*. Vol. 51. 1977.

Schlereth, Thomas J. *Artifacts and the American Past*. Nashville, Tennessee. American Association for State and Local History. 1980.

Schlereth, Thomas J. "It Wasn't that Simple". *Museum News*. January/February 1978.

Schlereth, Thomas J. (ed.) *Material Culture Studies in America*. Nashville, Tennessee. American Association for State and Local History. 1982.

Schlereth, Thomas J. "The Historic Museum Village as a Learning Environment". *The Museologist*. Vol. 141. 1977.

Schlereth, Thomas J.. "The History Behind, Within, and Outside the History Museum". *Curator*. Vol. 3. No. 4.1980.

Schmeisser, B. "The Population of Louisbourg: 1713-1758". *Manuscript Report No. 303*. Ottawa. Parks Canada. 1976.

Scottish Museums Council. *Museums Are For People*. Edinburg. Her Majesty's Stationary Office. 1985.

Screven, C.G. "Educational Evaluation and Research in Museums and Public Research: A Bibliography". *Curator*. Vo. 27. No.2. 1984.

Screven, C.G. "Exhibit Evaluation — a Goal Referenced Approach". *Curator*. Vol. 19. No. 3. 1976.

Screven, C.G. *The Measurement and Facilitation of Learning in the Museum Environment: an Experimental Analysis*. Washington. Smithsonian Institution. 1974.

Screven, C.G. "The Museum as a Responsive Learning Environment". *Museum News*. Vol. 47. No. 10. 1969.

Seale, W. *Recreating the Historic House Interior*. Nashville, Tennessee. American Association for State and Local History. 1979.

Sekers, David. "The Educational Potential of the Museum Shop". *Museums Journal*. Vol. 76. No. 4. 1977.

Silvester, J.W.H. "Exploiting Site Museums". *Museums Journal*. Vol. 75. No. 1. 1975.

Sukel, William M. "Museums as Organizations". *Curator*. Vol. 7. No. 4. 1974.

Stanton, J.E. "Communication and Communicators: Some Problems of Display". *Museum*. Vol. 35. No. 3. 1983.

Stearn, W.T. *The Natural History Museum at South Kensington: A History of the British Museum (Natural History)*. London. Heinemann. 1981.

Stillman, Diane et al. "A Focus for the Interdisciplinary Curriculum". *Museum News*. Vol. 61. No. 6. 1983.

Sukel, W.M. "MBO for Museums". *Museologist*. Vol. 139. 1976.

Skansen Open Air Museum. *Guide Books: Delsbo Farm, Eksharad Farmhouse, Finn Settlement, Iron-masters Farm, Lap Camp, Mora Farm, Seglora Church Belfries, Skogaholm Manor,Soldier's Cottage, Summer Farmstead from Alvdalen*. Stockholm. Skansen Open Air Museum. 1976.

Skansen Open Air Museum. *Skansen: A Short Guide For Visitors*. Stockholm. Skansen Open Air Museum. 1984.

Smith, E. Ann. "Glassware from a Reputed 1745 Siege Debris Context at the Fortress of Louisbourg". *History and Archaeology*. Ottawa. Parks Canada.1981.

Smith, Stuart. *A View from Iron Bridge*. Lancashire. The Ironbridge Gorge Museum Trust. 1979.

Stanley, George F.G. *New France: The Last Phase, 1744-1760*. Toronto. McClelland and Stewart. 1968.

Stansfield, Geoffrey. *Effective Interpretive Exhibitions*. Cheltenham. Countryside Commission. 1981.

Stansfield, Geoffrey & Woodhead, Peter. *Keyguide to Information Sources in Museum Studies*. London. Mansell. 1990.

Strong, Roy. "Thinking and Doing in the United Kingdom". *Museum*. No. 138 (Vol. XXXV. No. 2). 1983.

Thomson, G. *The Museum Environment*. London. Butterworths. 1978.

Tilden, Freeman. *Interpreting Our Heritage*. Chapel Hill, North Carolina. University of North Carolina Press. 1967.

Todish, Tim. "Fortress Louisbourg: The Gibraltar of North America." *Muzzleloader*. Vol. XIV. No. 2 (May-June 1987).

Toffler, Alvin. *The Third Wave*. New York. Morrow. 1980.

Tramposch, W.J. "Put there a Spark: How Colonial Williamsburg Trains Its Interpretive Crew". *History News*. Vol. 37. No. 7. 1982.

University College of Cape Breton. *The Forerunner*. Sydney, Nova Scotia. UCCB Division of Continuing Education. 1988.

Vauban, S. *Traite de Fortification*. Paris. (No publisher listed).1737.

Vergo, Peter (ed.). *The New Museology*. London. Reaktion Books. 1989.

Washburn, Wilcomb .E. *Defining the Museum's Purpose*. Cooperstown, New York. New York State Historical Association. 1975.

Wilcomb E. "The Museum's Responsibility in Adult Education". *Curator*. Vol. 7. No. 1. 1964.

Washburne, F.R. & J.A.Wager. "Evaluating Visitor Response to Exhibit Content". *Curator*. Vol.15. No. 3 (1972).

White, J.. *Visitors to the Ironbridge Gorge Museum 1980: An Analysis of a Visitor Survey*. Telford. Ironbridge Gorge Museum Trust. 1981.

Williams, D.T. *The Battle of Bosworth*. Leicester. Leicester University Press. 1973.

Wilson, M. *The Effective Management of Volunteer Programs*. Colorado. Volunteer Management. 1976.

Wittlin, A.S.. "Hazards of Communication by Exhibits". *Curator*. Vol. 14 No. 2. (1971).

Wittlin, A.S. *Museums: In Search of a Usable Future*. Cambridge, Massachussetts. MIT Press. 1970.

Wittlin, A.S.. "Two Missing Links in Museums: Communicators and Evaluators". *CMA Gazette*. Vol.12. No. 1. (1979).

Wrong, George M. (ed.). *Louisbourg in 1745: The Anonymous L'ettre D'un Habitant de Louisbourg, containing a narrative by an eye-witness of the siege in 1745*. Toronto. Warwick Bro's and Rutter. 1897.